POTOMAC
MARBLE

POTOMAC MARBLE

History of the Search for the Ideal Stone

PAUL KREINGOLD

THE
History
PRESS

Published by The History Press
Charleston, SC
www.historypress.com

Front cover, top left: courtesy Paul Kreingold; *center left and bottom*: courtesy the Architect of the Capitol.
All internal images are from the author's collection unless otherwise noted.

First published 2023

Manufactured in the United States

ISBN 9781467153171

Library of Congress Control Number: 2022947118

Notice: The information in this book is true and complete to the best of our knowledge. It is offered without guarantee on the part of the author or The History Press. The author and The History Press disclaim all liability in connection with the use of this book.

This book is dedicated to the unnamed stonecutters, stone carvers, marble cutters, polishers, drillers, shakers, blasters, marble masons, bricklayers, painters, plasterers, carpenters, joiners, boatmen, wheelwrights, blacksmiths, mechanics, pit sawyers, mule and oxen drivers and laborers, free and enslaved, whose brains and brawn built the Capital City. Although anonymous, their work ensures their immortality.

CONTENTS

Preface   9
Acknowledgements   11
Introduction   13

PART I. HISTORY
1. Benjamin Latrobe: Jefferson's Architect   17
2. The War of 1812 and the British Invasion   25
3. Burning Stone Buildings   29
4. Rebuild or Move the Capital City: The Return of Latrobe   32
5. The Battle for Potomac Marble   37
6. Latrobe's Potomac Marble Columns   43

PART II. CHARACTERISTICS OF POTOMAC MARBLE
7. Geology   49
8. Sinkholes   57
9. Caverns   61

PART III. THE SEARCH FOR THE QUARRIES
10. Background   83
11. Olde Izaak Walton Park   86
12. Leesburg Limestone Company   90
13. Finally, Success!   94
14. Confirmation by Contemporary Sources   105

Part IV. Rock Becomes Stone
15. Geologic Introduction   109
16. Quarrying Aquia Creek Sandstone   111
17. Quarrying Potomac Marble and More   119

Part V. The Quarry and the River
18. Ode to the Rivermen   135

Conclusion   139
Notes   147
Bibliography   161
Index   167
About the Author   171

PREFACE

*T*his manuscript is derived from the popular lecture that I first developed in 2018 and continue to deliver in Loudoun and surrounding counties. It also incorporates the article written for the C&O Canal Association website titled "Benjamin Latrobe's Potomac Marble Quarries." At the last count, the lecture has been presented in various iterations more than thirty times to libraries, senior centers and naturalist and conservation organizations.

Often, parts of the lecture are delivered on-site at the Latrobe quarry along the C&O Canal Towpath in Montgomery County, Maryland. Expeditions to this site include comments on Civil War history in the area by Poolesville historian and journalist Jon Wolz.

The author lecturing at the Loudoun County Izaak Walton League in January 2020.

I have written this manuscript for many reasons. The story it describes provides unusual insights into American history and its important actors at a time in our history that most Americans simply know nothing about. Furthermore, much that has been written about this subject is either partly true or untrue, and I hope to provide a corrective to that problem. Finally, I want to facilitate access to this historical material to future historians. In this written form, I have included quotations and other material that I think interesting and relevant but that were not included in the lecture for reasons of brevity.

ACKNOWLEDGEMENTS

When I began this project a few years ago, there were a few people who were quite supportive. Most of all, C&O Canal historian Karen Gray urged me to write up my research and edited my first published article, which appeared on the C&O Canal website. Thank you, Karen, for all your help.

My friend, historian and journalist Jon Wolz, has not only helped me lead a number of expeditions to Latrobe's quarry but also has done original work on the subject that I have included in this book. Along with our good friend rockhound Jim Kostka, we three have spent many hours exploring the quarries of our local area. Jim also taught me how to cut and polish Potomac Marble and has created some beautiful items from the stone in his workshop.

Other historians have also been generous with their time. Thank you to Robert Kapsch for a memorable lunch and to William C. Allen for a very supportive exchange of emails. Thank you to Mary and James Gage, who allowed me to use pictures from their nineteenth-century quarrying tools collection, offered advice on understanding quarry drill holes and generously led my family on a tour of granite quarries in Cape Ann, Massachusetts.

Thank you to architect and artist Richard Chenowith, who was kind enough to allow me to use his beautiful computer models of the old House of Representatives and his Statue of Liberty sculpture, for which I am very grateful.

A particular thanks to Mary Oehrlein, historic preservation officer at the Capitol (now retired), who provided me with invaluable documents and honored me by placing my early work in the Capitol Archive.

Jerrilynn Eby and Alaric MacGregor III, authors of *The Great Rock of Aquia*, spent a day with me and some friends touring the historical Virginia freestone quarries of Stafford County, Virginia. Their deep understanding of nineteenth-century quarries and quarrymen and their defense of Virginia Freestone against its detractors were fascinating and have informed this book, and I thank them.

My friend Valerie Rush was kind enough to apply her editing skills to the first iteration of this manuscript, and her complimentary remarks were much appreciated.

Thank you to Richard Welsh, Roger Biraben, Geoff Braunsberg, Karen Stone, George Lewis, David Crenshaw, Tom Caviness, John Adams, Paul Lawrence and Ed Spannaus and many others, each of whom made a valuable contribution to this work. And thank you to my wife, Linda, who has had to listen to me talk about Potomac Marble for the past five years and never complained.

Finally, I would like to thank the hundreds of people who have attended my lectures and expeditions over the years. It is the public's interest and curiosity about Potomac Marble that encouraged me to complete this project.

INTRODUCTION

ook at the picture of the rock below. It's not a particularly interesting rock. Perhaps if you were a ten-year-old (at heart), you might pick it up and throw it or kick it down the road, but really, it's just a rock. But have you ever thought about the difference between a rock and a stone? You wear a gem *stone*, not a gem *rock*. You pave with *stones*, not *rocks*. You build a *stone* wall, but you climb a *rock* wall.

So, what is the difference between a rock and a stone? Well, I'll tell you. If we humans take a rock and change it so it becomes useful or valuable, then it becomes a stone.[1]

Potomac Marble
as a rock.

This book, then, is the story of a short time in American history when Potomac Marble became a stone and ceased being a rock. The United States of America was at its lowest point in its short life, its Capital City razed and its government dispersed. At this historic nadir, Potomac Marble, as a stone, helped restore American pride and sovereignty—and then the stone's history was quickly forgotten.

My interest in Potomac Marble began a few years ago, when I was elected the conservation director of the Loudoun County Chapter of the Izaak Walton League of America. Tradition has it that the former grounds of the League, now Olde Izaak Walton Park in Leesburg, Virginia, was one of the sources of the Potomac Marble for the Capitol. Intrigued by this story, I began to research the subject.

Suddenly, I found myself in the early nineteenth century reading the letters of Thomas Jefferson, James Madison, James Monroe and Benjamin Latrobe. I found myself in an America at war, an America building canals and steamboats and, importantly, an America developing its own notions of beauty.

The story begins with Benjamin H. Latrobe.

PART I

HISTORY

But suppose it to last a century, what is a century in the life of nations?

—*Benjamin Latrobe, March 31, 1817*

Chapter 1

BENJAMIN LATROBE

JEFFERSON'S ARCHITECT

Benjamin H. Latrobe was born in Yorkshire, England, in 1764. His family was of the Moravian faith, giving him access to some of the best educational institutions in both England and Germany. By the time he left school, he spoke English, German, French, Italian, Greek, Hebrew and Latin and was a competent musician, artist and engineer. After graduation, he took a job with a leading engineering firm in London, working on, among other things, the Basingstoke Canal.[2] It was in architecture, though, that he planned a career. He immigrated to the United States in 1795 for many reasons, one being that he was a supporter of America's republican experiment.[3] This was a place where architects did not yet practice, and here his conception of architecture based on Classical Greek forms could flourish. In doing so, he became the father of American architecture. (See his picture on page 65.)

Latrobe was a brilliant and charming individual. As the architect and historian Richard Chenowith describes him, he was

> *a man who could swing from melancholic and desperate in the travails of his life, to powerfully optimistic and self-assured in his successes; he could be savagely satirical and wickedly funny when describing the absurdities of life he encountered. But he was also intensely analytical. He could write extemporaneously on the sciences—structure, geology, hydrology, navigation—and also could ruminate tirelessly on music, art, people, and current events. He's even credited with writing the first description of jazz music, which he had heard in New Orleans late in his life.[4]*

Wherever he went in America, people were drawn to his genius. He was soon tuning pianos, leading choruses and designing houses, prisons and concert halls. In July 1796, Latrobe visited President George Washington at Mount Vernon. The famous Revolutionary general had grown quite weary by then of "guests" just dropping in, uninvited, to greet "the Great Man." Usually, he gave these "guests" a quick lunch and sent them on their way, but when Latrobe arrived, he was asked to stay for two days. Among the items discussed was canal building. Latrobe wrote, "The conversation then turned upon the rivers of Virginia. He gave me a very minute account of all their directions, their natural advantages, and what he conceived might be done for their improvement by art."[5] Latrobe was familiar with canal technology from his work in London, and the president was eager to gather whatever knowledge he could in furtherance of his Potomac River improvement plan, which plays an important part in this story and which I will discuss later.[6]

Seeking more opportunities, Latrobe moved from Norfolk, Virginia, his landing place, to Richmond, Virginia, and then to the largest and most cosmopolitan city in the country at that time: Philadelphia.

Arriving in Philadelphia in 1798, Latrobe was commissioned to build America's first Neoclassical building, the Bank of Pennsylvania. He was soon contracted to provide a water supply for the city. Using two steam engines,[7] at a time when there may have been only two others on the whole continent, Latrobe pumped water out of the Schuylkill River into a reservoir. From the reservoir, another steam engine pumped the water into a seventeen-thousand-gallon wooden holding tank, which provided water pressure for the system via gravity and thence to hydrants throughout the city, all connected with thirty thousand feet of wooden pipes. On January 26, 1802, Latrobe lit the fire under the two steam engine boilers, and soon, because the hydrants were deliberately left open, clean, potable water poured out of every hydrant in Philadelphia.[8] Imagine that!

Latrobe attracted the attention of the American Philosophical Society. Founded by Benjamin Franklin early in the previous century, the society had served its purpose well, bringing together the greatest minds in America in promotion of arts and sciences. I am often asked why Franklin called his organization the American *Philosophical* Society and not the American *Scientific* Society or the Society for *Arts* and *Sciences*. This is because before the modern proliferation of scientific specialization, these men (and eventually women)[9] considered themselves "Natural Philosophers." The Greek meaning of the word *philosophy* is "lover of wisdom," and these lovers of wisdom proposed to explore and understand *all* of God's creation. Latrobe was elected to join on

July 19, 1799, and as a natural philosopher, he submitted papers on geology, botany and anthropology.[10] As I said, the natural philosophers explored *all* of God's creation.

It was in the American Philosophical Society that Latrobe met Thomas Jefferson, another member, in 1798.[11] After Jefferson became president, he invited Latrobe on March 15, 1803, to become Washington, D.C.'s head architect, the surveyor of public buildings, at a salary of $1,700 per year.[12] In doing so, he appointed the "first professional architect and engineer to work in America."[13] Latrobe was now tasked with finally finishing the long-delayed capital city, Washington, D.C.[14]

The Capital City had been through many architects since George Washington approved final plans and laid the cornerstone on September 18, 1793, but unlike the White House, the Capitol was still unfinished. Through Jefferson's two terms as president, he and Latrobe formed an uneasy but productive partnership.

It was uneasy for many reasons. The two men were from different generations. Latrobe was in his late thirties and Jefferson in his early sixties. They also had different notions of esthetics. In a letter to Jefferson, Latrobe writes, "My *principles* of good taste are rigid in Grecian architecture. I am a bigoted Greek in the condemnation of Roman architecture of Ballbec, Palmyra and Spalatro."[15] His architectural bible was *Antiquities of Athens*, published in 1762 and available at the Philadelphia Library Company.[16] He believed that the beautiful art of Greece was the result of the freedom it afforded its citizens: "The Apollo of Phidias, the Venus of Praxiteles, the group of Laocoon, are in fact monuments not more of the arts, than of the freedom of Greece."[17] He thought very little of Roman art and architecture, whose only bright moments copied from the Greeks. Most importantly, art and architecture for Latrobe was an imperative question of growing and preserving his adopted republican homeland. Art would flourish as the republican experiment flourished, as its morals and outlooks remained enlightened. It would die if the Republic became decadent, as it did in Greece:

> *Greece, indeed, at last, lost her freedom; she lost it when she lost her virtue; she lost it when she prostituted the fine arts to the gratification of vice; when her music...sounded only to guide the steps of licentiousness, she lost it when her sculpture and painting, instead of immortalizing the forms of her heroes and philosophers, and rendering her gods adorable, became the sycophants of wealth and the slaves of sensuality; then, to use the language of Pliny, not less forcible than true, the arts ceased in Greece.*[18]

Latrobe did not want to build classic temples to Zeus but rather beautiful buildings for the efficient operation of an enlightened republican government and believed that such buildings could only be accomplished in the classic style. As author Jean Baker wrote, "Latrobe intended architectural expressions in a new style worthy of a nation rebuilding the world politically, inspired but not dictated by the past."[19] He complained of Jefferson, "I am cramped in this design by his prejudices in favor of the old French books, out of which he fishes everything,"[20] and how he "seems in many cases to have attempted to force the state of things into the mold of his theories."[21] In other words, in Latrobe's mind, Jefferson was perhaps a bit of an "old fogey."

Nevertheless, their collaboration produced a wonderful building that was, as Latrobe's biographer Hamlin put it, "undoubtedly the most beautiful legislative chamber in the Western world."[22]

Look at the picture of the Capitol in 1812 on page 65. The building on the left or north side contained the Senate Chamber, Supreme Court and the Library of Congress.[23] On the right or south side was the House of Representatives Chamber, and in the center, where the dome is now, was a wooden walkway connecting the two buildings.

Unfortunately, we have little idea what the inside actually looked like. Photography was not yet invented, and no paintings were done. Fortunately, architect and architectural historian Richard Chenoweth, in an article titled "The Most Beautiful Room in the World,"[24] has re-created the room for us using a computer model based on whatever scraps of information he could gather. Let's examine this model, which appears on page 66.

The first thing you will notice is the ceiling, which consisted of one hundred glass blocks each sixteen inches thick. Note that from the standpoint of early nineteenth-century architecture, the fact that the ceiling was "only" sixteen inches thick was considered quite astonishing.[25] These glass panels were Jefferson's idea. He had first seen such a roof not in "old French books" but in a French grain market in Paris and insisted on copying them here. Latrobe was against the glass panels. There were no modern caulking materials at this time, no plastics or petroleum-based products. Caulking came from pine sap, and Latrobe knew it would leak, as it did. Latrobe also thought the lighting resulting from these panels would diffuse itself in different patterns and intensities through the course of the day, creating a distraction for the representatives. His preference was a lantern or cupola centered on the top of the dome allowing a constant and diffused light.[26]

Jefferson won that fight; after all, he was the president! The United States had no capability to produce such glass, so one hundred glass panels were ordered from Germany. When they failed to arrive, they were reordered from Great Britain.[27]

The domed ceiling rested on twenty-six-foot-eight-inch-high fluted Corinthian columns. The sandstone for these columns was quarried from the Aquia Creek Quarries, which I will discuss later.

Notice the red curtains hanging between each column. When the congressmen began to use the room, they complained that echoes made it difficult to hear the speaker. Latrobe, one of the first to study acoustics,[28] had these curtains, each twenty feet long, hung between the columns to dampen the echoes.[29]

The Statue of Liberty behind the Speaker's platform and the giant bald eagle over the Speaker's platform point to one of Latrobe's many problems in completing this hall. In the United States at that time, there were no stone sculptors, although there was in New York City a quite competent wood carver named William Rust.[30] To address this problem, Congress authorized money to import two Italian marble sculptors and their families. Giuseppe Franzoni and Giovanni Andrei arrived in 1806.

Franzoni was given the task of carving a giant American bald eagle with a twelve-and-a-half-foot wingspan. As Franzoni commenced to work, Latrobe noticed that he was carving a European eagle and not an American one. How could Franzoni know the difference? He had just arrived on this continent.

To solve this problem, Latrobe contacted his friend and fellow American Philosophical Society member artist Charles Wilson Peale. He wrote Peale on April 18, 1806:

> *My Dear Sir: You will say, and I am afraid with truth, that I never write to you but to give you trouble. At present I have really no other object but to lay myself under still greater obligations to your kindness than I am already.*
>
> *In my design of the Hall of the House of Representatives, an eagle has become necessary as the principal decoration of the center of the Hall in the frieze....*
>
> *We have here two most capital Italian sculptors lately arrived. One of them is now modeling an eagle, but it is an Italian, or Roman, or Greek eagle, and I want an American Bald-eagle. May I therefore beg the favor of you to request one of your very obliging, and skilful sons, to send me a drawing of the head and claws of the bald-eagle of his general proportions*

with the wings extended, and especially of the arrangement of the feathers below the wing when extended. The eagle will be fourteen feet, from tip to tip of the wings, so that any glaring impropriety of character will be immediately detected by our Western members.

Let me beg of you to do me this favor. I want merely outlines, but as soon as possible. I should be truly thankful

Yours very affectionately, B.H. Latrobe[31]

Charles Wilson Peale had eleven children, four of whom he named Rembrandt, Titian, Raphael and Rubens. Peale is known today as one of the great American portrait artists of his age, but he also had a Museum of Curiosities in Philadelphia where he displayed specimens of American wildlife and fine paintings. The most popular exhibit was a complete mastodon skeleton unearthed in New York State. The purpose of the museum was not remunerative, and the entrance fee was low. Rather, its purpose was, in line with the American Philosophical Association's tenets, the diffusion of knowledge. In his delightful self-portrait on page 66, Peale "lifts the curtain," revealing shelves of specimens, with paintings above them and the mastodon skeleton just behind the curtain. More importantly, notice that there are not only men but also women and children looking at and learning from the exhibits.

Getting back to our eagle story, about a week after Latrobe requested an eagle drawing from Peale, a carriage arrived in Washington, D.C., with a big box on it addressed to Latrobe. Inside was the preserved head and claws of an American bald eagle. Franzoni could now continue his work.[32]

Richard Chenoweth has also provided us with a beautiful reproduction of Franzoni's Statue of Liberty sculpted in clay. As Chenoweth points out, Liberty is dressed in modern clothing and not the classical garb of the French Statue of Liberty now in New York Harbor. In her right hand, she holds a scroll, the U.S. Constitution, and in her left hand a liberty cap. Fittingly, her right foot is stepping on a crown. For a complete analysis of this statue, refer to his article "The Very First Miss Liberty Latrobe, Franzoni and the first Statue of Liberty, 1807–1814" in *Le Libellio d'AEGI* magazine.[33]

As war fever grew in 1811 and 1812, money for continued work on the Capitol was no longer forthcoming from Congress. Latrobe left Washington, D.C., for, hopefully, greener pastures. He received an upbeat letter from Jefferson on July 12, 1812, congratulating him on the achievements of their partnership:

Reproduction of Franzoni's Statue of Liberty by Richard Chenoweth, a sculpture in clay. Liberty holds the Constitution in her right hand and a liberty cap in her left, and her right foot rests on a royal crown. *Courtesy of Richard Chenoweth.*

I shall live in the hope that the day will come when an opportunity will be given you of finishing the middle building in a style worthy of the two wings and worthy of the first temple dedicated to the sovereignty of the people, embellishing with Athenian taste the course of a nation looking far beyond the range of Athenian destinies.[34]

But the frustration after his years in the Capital City, despite his successes, is clear in a letter Latrobe wrote to his friend Nathaniel Ingraham[35] on September 9, 1813:

Bidding an eternal adieu to the malice, backbiting, and slander, trickery, fraud & hypocrisy, lofty pretensions & scanty means, boasts of patriotism & bargaining of conscience, pretense of religion and breach of her laws, starving doctors, thriving attorneys, whitewashing jail oaths, upstart haughtiness, & depressed merit, & five thousand other nuisances that constitute the very essence of this community. You can stand a little vulgarity, therefore I say with Sancho, the more You stir it the more it stinketh.[36]

Putting aside Latrobe's sour view of Washington, D.C., look again at the computer-generated model of the first iteration of the House of Representatives Chamber designed by Jefferson and Latrobe. It is, without a doubt, beautiful.

And then it all came to an end.

Chapter 2

THE WAR OF 1812 AND THE BRITISH INVASION

*T*he first two years of the War of 1812 took a desultory form in the Potomac River and Chesapeake Bay area. The British, mainly concerned with defeating Napoleon in Europe, sent Rear Admiral George Cockburn on what was basically a harassment mission. Cockburn attacked, looted and burned the tobacco plantations up and down the river and bay, killing anyone who resisted. He was condemned by Americans as a "brutal monster" and "a disgrace to England and human nature."[37]

Cockburn also took advantage of the greatest weakness of the plantation system in Virginia and Maryland: the slave system. Plantation owners knew that their slaves were a dangerous "internal enemy"[38] and were terrified of a slave uprising. In fact, men were not recruited from this area for the war against the British because it was understood that to prevent a possible slave rebellion, they had to remain at home.[39] The British advertised through word of mouth that they would free any slave who escaped to their ships. During the day, to announce their presence, British ships sailed up and down the coast with their bands playing. At night, they lit up their masts and yardarms, making themselves visible to those who could steal a boat and escape. Learning that an escaped father would not leave without his wife and children, they accepted whole families. Over three thousand slaves did escape, and as opposed to the Revolution, when British promises of freedom were often lies,[40] the British kept their word. Former slaves were recruited to the British navy or resettled in Canada. Indeed, four hundred former enslaved men were formed into an effective militia that either attacked plantations on their own or led British troops on raids.[41]

The British were very chary of a full invasion of their former colonies. Having been defeated at Saratoga and Yorktown during the Revolution, they remembered suffering huge losses even in engagements they had considered victories, such as Bunker Hill. Logistics were also a problem. During the Revolution, despite the fact that the forests of North America stretched thousands of miles to the west, the British had to import firewood from Europe. And despite the fact that the former colonies had a huge population of horses, they had to import horses from Holland. They even had to import forage for their horses, and it took two horses pulling a wagon to feed three horses on a daily basis. In other words, it took two horses to feed one cavalry horse. All of this because the American army and militias denied them access to their rich forests and farmlands.[42]

Everything changed, though, in spring of 1814. In March of that year, Napoleon abdicated and was sent into exile on Elba Island. Suddenly, the British had troops and resources available—troops with which they could teach these American upstarts a real lesson.

On August 19, 1814, 4,500 troops under the command of General Robert Ross sailed up the Patuxent River and landed at Benedict, Maryland. These were battle-hardened troops, proud to have defeated Napoleon and resentful that the Americans, or "rebels" as they called them, were not allies in the war against Napoleon. For many of the officers, this was a chance to get revenge for the devastating defeat at Yorktown thirty-three years earlier. Indeed, the brother of the British commander-in-chief of North American operations, Vice Admiral Alexander Cochrane, had been killed at Yorktown.[43]

As I like to say, these 4,500 British troops weren't just troops but TROOPS! As they left the ships that hot and humid August morning, dressed in fine wool jackets, linen shirts and hemp trousers,[44] they sang the latest hit song in London, drawn from Handel's *Judas Maccabeus* oratorio: "See, the conqu'ring hero come—Sound the trumpets! Beat the drums!—Sports prepare! The laurel bring! Songs of triumph to him sing!"[45] As they marched, unopposed, dozens collapsed from the one-hundred-degree heat,[46] and Cochrane wrote, "The Worst Enemy we have to contend with is the climate,"[47] which anyone who has experienced an August day in Maryland or Virginia can understand.

In Washington,[48] meanwhile, there was panic and looting. People left the city for safety in the countryside, taking as much as they could carry. An account of that time by Senate clerk Lewis Machen gives us a sense of the Capital City as the British approached:

British Advance on Washington, 1814

Map of the British invasion routes in 1814. *National Park Service.*

Before the destruction of the Capitol by the British, all in the City was doubt, confusion, and dismay. The citizens were absent, under arms; business was suspended. Every means of transportation was either engaged or in use; and no certain intelligence of the Enemy was either communicated or known. [49]

There was one family, though, that stayed to welcome the British. Ironically, Martha Custis Peter, the granddaughter of Martha Washington, was such an anglophile that she named her house Tudor Place and her daughter Britannia. [50]

Secretary of War John Armstrong, however, declared that the British would never invade Washington but were headed for Baltimore: "By God, they would not come with such a fleet without meaning to strike somewhere. But they certainly will not come here! What the devil will they do here? No! No! Baltimore is the place, Sir. That is of so much more consequence." [51]

With this belief, he discouraged his clerks from saving critical historical documents threatened with British despoilation. The brave clerks ignored their boss and packed up Washington's resignation letter, the Declaration of Independence and other documents and secreted them in Virginia.

President Madison, doubting the veracity of his war secretary as well, decided to send a spy to see what the enemy was actually doing. Who did he send as a spy? There was no Central Intelligence Agency in those times, so he sent his secretary of state, James Monroe. Monroe jumped on a horse and, accompanied by twenty-five militiamen, galloped the fifty miles to the hills overlooking Benedict. Halfway there, Monroe realized he had forgotten his telescope but continued on nevertheless. Seeing that the British were on the march, he rode back to the president and confirmed that they were on their way to Washington.[52]

In retrospect, it is really not a surprise that Monroe was sent out as a spy. He was sixty-six years old in 1814, healthy and no shrinking violet. In fact, back in 1776, he had crossed the Delaware River with George Washington, was wounded at the Battle of Trenton and later survived the terrible winter at Valley Forge in 1777–78.

President Madison organized a last stand to hold off the British at Bladensburg, Maryland, on August 24. The president and his cabinet were present on the battlefield (!) until it was clear that the British, despite tremendous casualties, would sweep the American militia from the field. With no one blocking their way, the British entered Washington in the late afternoon of August 24, 1814. At 9:06 p.m., they began burning the Capitol. (See page 67.)

Chapter 3

BURNING STONE BUILDINGS

I have often been asked, "How do you burn a stone building?" Well, to understand that, we have to take a short detour to the eighteenth-century colonization of India by the British.

As the British attempted to colonize the Indian subcontinent, they met stiff resistance from various political entities. Among those was the Kingdom of Mysore located in the south of India. The British fought four wars against Mysore where the kingdom defended itself with metal rockets that could travel over one mile. These rockets were not particularly accurate, but they could wreak havoc on troops and were far advanced of anything in the British arsenal. After the Fourth Mysore War in 1799, the British captured some of these rockets and assigned scientist William Congreve to make them more accurate and more deadly, a task he accomplished so well that the Congreve Rocket was used extensively in the Napoleonic Wars a few years later. In fact, when the British landed at Benedict, Maryland, in 1814, among their ships were "rocket ships." These were not the rocket ships we are familiar with today but wooden ships used as platforms to launch rockets.[53]

Invading the beautiful House of Representatives, the collaborative effort of Jefferson and Latrobe, the British troops first shot Congreve rockets at the ceiling. Remember that the ceiling was sixteen inches thick with one hundred embedded glass blocks. The rockets made a mess but failed to bring down the roof. Next, they gathered wooden desks and chairs and the twenty-foot-long acoustical curtains and piled them in the center of the hall. Breaking open forty-pound Congreve rockets, they dumped the black powder on top of the flammables and lit the fire.

The fire soon burned so hot that the glass blocks melted and the fluted Aquia Creek sandstone columns began a process of calcination, basically disintegrating.

Over on the Senate side, the British found a ready supply of combustibles—the Library of Congress—which was burned along with the furniture. Ironically, most of the books burned by the soldiers were British.[54]

In a letter to Thomas Jefferson on July 12, 1815, Latrobe described the destruction done by the conflagration:

> *In the house of Representatives, the devastation has been dreadful. There was no want of materials for conflagration. In 1811, when the number of members of Congress was increased the old platform was left in its place and another raised over it giving additional quantity of dry loose lumber. All the stages and seats of the Galleries were of timber and yellow pine. The Mahagony furniture, desk, tables and Chairs were in their places. At first, they fired Rockets through the Roof. But they did not set fire to it; they sent men on to it, but it was covered with Sheet Iron. At last, they made a great pile in the Center of the room of furniture and retiring, set fire to a large quantity of Rocket stuff in the middle. The whole was soon in a blaze and so intense was the flame that the Glass and Lights was melted, and I have now lumps weighing many pounds of glass, run into the Mass. The stone, is like most freestone, unable to resist the force of flame. But I believe no known material could have withstood the effects of so sudden and intense heat.*[55]

The British also burned the White House and other government buildings, while we burned our own Navy Yard to keep thousands of pounds of naval supplies and ships from the hands of the enemy. The fire burned so brightly that citizens of Leesburg, Virginia, forty-five miles to the west, could see the glow.[56] It is said that only a fortuitous rainstorm quenched the fire after much damage.

In his sixth Annual Message to Congress on November 20, 1814, President Madison set the tone for the patriotic reaction throughout the nation. Speaking of Britain, he wrote:

> *He has avowed his purpose of trampling on the usages of civilized warfare, and given earnests of it in the plunder and wanton destruction of private*

*property. * * * His barbarous policy has not even spared those monuments of the arts and models of taste with which the country had enriched and embellished its infant metropolis. From such an adversary hostility in its greatest force and in its worst forms may be looked for. The American people will face it with the undaunted spirit which in their revolutionary struggle defeated his unrighteous projects. His threats and his barbarities, instead of dismay, will kindle in every bosom an indignation not to be extinguished but in the disaster and expulsion of such cruel invaders.*[57]

There was some British sentiment against this wanton destruction. The *London Statesman*, referring to the recent occupation of Paris by allied armies, including Russians, wrote, "The Cossacks spared Paris, but we spared not the Capitol of America."[58] General Ross, on learning that the books of the Library of Congress had been destroyed, expressed his regret, remarking that he did not "make war…against letters,"[59] and one of Vice Admiral Cochrane's lieutenants is reported to have said it was "a pity to burn anything so beautiful."[60]

There were, however, few reservations on the part of most British officers to this desecration of some of the most beautiful buildings in existence. In fact, Vice Admiral Cochrane gave orders "to destroy and lay waste to such towns and districts upon the coast as you may find assailable,"[61] and Cockburn believed that burning cities was a very good way to demoralize the enemy.[62]

And then, as poet Philip Freneau wrote:

> *A veteran host, by veterans led,*
> *With Ross and Cockburn at their head,*
> *They came—they saw—they burn'd—and fled.*[63]

To where did they flee? To Baltimore, where they were far from triumphant. On September 12, General Ross was killed in battle, and because of the courageous stand of Fort McHenry on September 14, the British were unable to capture the Monumental City.[64]

As you probably know, Francis Scott Key, witnessing this battle from a prison ship in the harbor, wrote "The Star-Spangled Banner." And as I like to say, "Despite the *Congreve* rockets' red glare, and the bombs bursting in air," the proud British army and navy were defeated.

On February 18, 1815, the Treaty of Ghent was signed, ending the War of 1812.[65]

Chapter 4

REBUILD OR MOVE THE CAPITAL CITY

THE RETURN OF LATROBE

*O*n October 20, 1814, Congress began its debate on rebuilding the Capital City. They formed a select committee whose purpose was "to inquire into the expediency of rebuilding or repairing the President's house, Capitol, and public offices, and of the expense necessary for that purpose, and whether the public interest or convenience would be promoted by any change or alteration of the sites of said buildings."[66]

As you can imagine, many local interests wanted the capital moved to their town or city. Others wanted to spend as little as possible to get the government functioning again.[67] Senator Eligius Fromentin, a Democratic-Republican from Louisiana, expressed his objections to a rebuild in this way on February 3, 1815:

> *Provide for filling the ranks of your Army; provide for clothing, feeding, and paying, your soldiers and sailors. Instead of borrowing money for building costly edifices, borrow money for protecting against an invading foe the edifices yet standing. Drive the enemy from the country; then, indeed, my pride will be satisfied; then I will, with pleasure, vote money, as much money as you please, for rebuilding our public edifices; and then the more magnificent the plan, the more elegant its execution, the more my pride will be gratified.*[68]

Ultimately, it was one man, dead since 1799, whose voice decided this question. It was George Washington's imprimatur that saved Washington, D.C. As Congressman Joseph Lewis, a Virginia Federalist, said in his speech during the debate, "He [Washington] actually came upon the ground, and marked the very spots upon which the buildings were to be placed."

Lewis continued:

> *He would not be compelled by an act of the enemy to abandon, or change in the smallest degree, any of the plans of the public edifices they had destroyed. He would rebuild them precisely on the same ground; not a stone or brick should be changed, but they should be finished in a style of increased magnificence and grandeur. It never should be said, because the enemy had destroyed our Capitol, that Congress were afraid to rebuild it, lest it might again be destroyed.*[69]

> *What that man [Washington] has done let no mortal attempt to undo. His ways are not to be mended by man.*[70]

Lewis also reminded Congress of the financial considerations:

> *We have been told, that large quantities of our public stock have been lately sent to Holland for sale. Is it to be believed, sir, with a knowledge of what we are about to do, (for it is in that country that our city lots have been sold, and held as security for money borrowed,) that they will trust us for a cent, when everything which they deemed sacred is thus violated?*[71]

In addition, the Washington, D.C. banks, eager to maintain the land value of their investments and mortgages, offered a $500,000 rebuilding loan at 6 percent.

> *The committee think it not irrelative to the object of their inquiries, though it is not specifically enjoined, to state also that the several banks within the District of Columbia, desirous of facilitating an object so interesting to the district, have made a formal and binding offer in writing, to advance on loan to the Government, upon reasonable terms, the sum of $500,000, to be applied exclusively to the purpose of rebuilding or repairing the President's house, Capitol, or public offices.*[72]

On February 9, 1815, Congress voted to stay in the city. The vote was 77 to 55—that is, a mere 12 votes decided the issue. If those votes had gone in another direction, we would have had a new capital city somewhere else in America.

On February 13, 1815, Congress passed "An Act Making Appropriations for Repairing or Rebuilding the Public Buildings within the City of Washington":

> *Be it enacted by the Senate and House of Representatives of the United States of America in Congress assembled, That the President of the United States cause to be repaired or rebuilt forthwith, the President's House, Capitol and public offices, on their present sites in the city of Washington, and that he be authorized to borrow, at an interest not exceeding six per centum per annum, from any bank or banks within the District of Columbia, or from any individual or individuals, a sum not exceeding five hundred thousand dollars, to be applied exclusively to that object.*[73]

The search for an architect began.

WHERE WAS BENJAMIN LATROBE?

As the war threat grew in 1811, the funding for further construction of the Capital City dried up, and Latrobe was offered a job by another member of the American Philosophical Society, Robert Fulton. The job was directing the construction of a fleet of steamboats in Pittsburgh, Pennsylvania, for the Ohio–Mississippi river trade. Latrobe realized that if he was successful, his family's fortune and security would be assured.

Unfortunately, it turned out to be a disaster, and Fulton soon pulled out his money. At one point, Latrobe wrote to a friend, "We…have eaten up part of our furniture."[74] Out of money, the Latrobe family survived by selling their furniture.

It is at this point that Latrobe succumbed to depression. He sat for days in a dark room, uncommunicative. His wife, Mary, refused to admit defeat and launched a campaign to get her husband the job in Washington. More research should be done on Mary Latrobe, who was a brilliant and talented woman in her own right, an accomplished singer and musician who played what we would call classical guitar. For Mary, of course, the music wasn't "classical." After all, Mozart had died only twenty years earlier, and at that very time, Beethoven was writing his opera *Fidelio*.

Philadelphia-born Mary had powerful friends whom she had cultivated during the years the family lived in Washington, D.C. There, Mary and Benjamin had hosted soirees at their house, inviting the intellectual and cultural leaders of the city and the nation, including diplomats, politicians, artists and scientists. When President Madison's wife, Dolley, needed to decorate the White House, it was Benjamin and Mary who helped her choose the furniture. In fact, along with everything else that was destroyed as the White House burned were a guitar and pianoforte chosen for Dolley by Mary.[75]

Mary opened her campaign with a letter to Dolley Madison, a lifelong friend whose judgment and acumen were trusted by her husband, the sitting president. She wrote to others of influence as well, and on March 15, 1815, President Madison offered Latrobe the job of rebuilding the Capitol building.

Mary relates the scene in her memoirs quoted in Hamlin's Latrobe biography. She received

> *a large Packet with the President's seal, containing a recall for my husband to resume his former situation—never can I forget the transport I felt in going to him as he reclined in deep depression in an easy chair. I presented him the Packet. Behold, I said, what Providence has done for you! And what your poor weak wife has been made the humble instrument in obtaining. He threw himself on my breast and wept like a child—so true it is that women can bear many trials better than men![76]*

His appointment was a step down from his prewar position as surveyor of public buildings, where he had been responsible for all public building

Latrobe sketch: "Leesburg Courthouse, May 10, 1815—barbaric version of the Tuscan order." *Courtesy of the Maryland Center for History and Culture.*

in Washington, D.C. Instead, he was appointed architect of the Capitol only. Within a year, the office of commissioner became vacant, and Latrobe urged President Madison to appoint him. The president ignored his pleas and appointed Secretary of State Monroe's longtime friend Samuel Lane to that position. Latrobe was no longer working directly with the president and Congress, as he had with Jefferson; now he had a boss, Lane, who mediated his relationships with those two institutions. Nevertheless, he accepted the offer, and the family prepared to move back to Washington, D.C.

On the way to the Capital City, Latrobe passed through Leesburg, Virginia (my hometown). There he sketched the Leesburg Courthouse. Latrobe noted on the drawing that the building was a "barbaric version of the Tuscan order."[77] Today's citizens of Leesburg will be happy to know that the building he was criticizing was a previous version of their courthouse and is no longer standing. I am not sure what Latrobe would say about the current courthouse, but all that is remaining from that previous iteration are some of the Tuscan columns' pedestals in the grass in front of the building.

Chapter 5

THE BATTLE FOR POTOMAC MARBLE

After an initial trip to Washington in April 1815, the Latrobe family permanently settled in the city on June 30. Viewing the Capitol's remains, Latrobe declared it "a magnificent ruin."[78] The building was covered with graffiti reading, among others, "James Madison is a rascal, a coward and a fool," reflecting some of the public's belief that the president had not sufficiently defended the Capitol from the British.[79] Globs of melted glass from Jefferson's ceiling littered the floor. In some places, the sandstone subjected to great heat had disintegrated. Interestingly, Latrobe wrote, "The only fact that I regret deeply, is the destruction of our national Records. Everything else money can replace."[80] Later, on May 7, 1816, he wrote to his sister that his plan for the buildings was to "restore them infinitely more splendidly than they existed before the Invasion of the Goths."[81]

There was general agreement among President Madison and Congress that the new Capitol must be more magnificent than the old. After all, if an enemy burns your Capital City, it is not enough to rebuild it. You must show the enemy that you are not defeated and demoralized but stronger than ever. In light of this, there was an agreement that the building should use American materials as much as possible and not imported stone from Europe, which was often less expensive because of the primitive nature of transport in the country at the time.

Remember, Latrobe and the Founding Fathers were classically educated. It was the Parthenon in Athens that was their model for public works, and

"Original Capitol After the Fire of 1814," from drawing after Chittenden. *Architect of the Capitol.*

the Parthenon's columns are marble. Latrobe had become aware of Potomac Marble many years earlier, but "the pressures of work" prevented him from using it, and now, he was determined to do so.[82]

In a report to the Committee on Public Buildings on November 28, 1816, he described a stone that is a "very hard but beautiful marble" that "has been proved to answer every expectation that was formed, not only of its beauty, but of its capacity to furnish columns of any length, and to be applicable to any purpose to which colored marble can be applied."[83] On March 13, 1816, Latrobe set out to visit quarries in Loudoun and Montgomery Counties. Traveling with John Hartnet, "an experienced marble mason,"[84] he searched for the quarry with the most beautiful stone and the best transportation access. This was the first of many visits to the quarries. For example, Samuel Lane, the commissioner of public buildings, reported the following expenses to Congress on December 12, 1816:

Date: May 21, 1816
To Whom Paid: B. Henry Latrobe
On what account: Expenses exploring marble quarries
Amount: $161.72

Date: August 14th, 1816
To Whom Paid: John Carnes
On what account: Hack hire to marble quarries
Amount: 16.00[85]

As a result of these investigations, a contract was signed in April 1816 with Samuel Clapham, owner of land along the Potomac, and John Hartnet was contracted to produce twenty-two columns for the House Chamber at the price of $1,550 each.[86] Additionally, twelve more columns and eighteen pilasters would be needed for the Senate.[87]

This quickly proved to be a poor arrangement, and the government was forced to take over and run the quarry itself. President Monroe replaced Hartnet with Robert Leckie, an experienced quarrier, and Hartnet, the marble mason, was put in charge of cutting and polishing the quarried stone once it reached Washington.

The following is an extract from a letter written by Samuel Lane in 1818 to the Committee on Expenditures of the Public Buildings describing the quarry start-up problems:

> *A contract was therefore entered into with a marble mason for the columns required, at $1,550 each, delivered in this city; and a sum of money advanced, upon security, to the contractor. But the difficulties and expenses attending an enterprise of this kind proved to be greater than had been calculated upon. In short, the money advanced and the private resources of the contractor were expended before much progress had been made at the quarry, and the contractor being unable to give such security as would authorize further advances, to the extent which might be required, it became necessary to abandon the undertaking altogether, or to adopt some other mode of carrying it into effect.*
>
> *After a full investigation of the state of the quarry by persons of science and skill, and a consideration of all the circumstances connected with this subject, it was thought best to prosecute the works at the quarry; and, as no contractor of responsibility could be procured, this could only be done by employing artists and hands on the public account. These inquiries, and the necessary arrangements with the owner and the lessees of the quarry, were not completed until the later end of March last.*[88]

Progress at the quarry went very slowly for many reasons. It was "worked by inexperienced crews who lost eighty tons of marble before they learned the proper way to cut and split rock. Sometimes the Potomac River was too low for boats to ferry the marble. At other times, flood waters swirled six feet deep in the stonecutters' sheds....In winter, the workers' feet froze.... Brawling, gambling, and drunkenness caused further delays."[89]

On March 4, 1817, President Monroe was inaugurated. The new president was determined to get the Capitol completed, and Benjamin Latrobe found himself engaged in a battle for Potomac Marble aided by an impatient president.

On the same day as his inauguration, Monroe met with the government's master stonecutter, George Blagden. Blagden insisted that Potomac Marble should not be used for the Capitol's columns because, he claimed, it could not be cut and polished and could not bear its own weight. In a letter to Jefferson, Latrobe described how he countered Blagden's objections:

> He [Blagden] *reported in writing, that the stone would not bear its own weight, when* lewis'ed.[90] *I immediately suspended by a small Lewis a block of 2 ton weight in the Capitol. He then doubted whether it could be wrought,—& to try the experiment, a small Column 3 inches in diameter* which had been wrought and polished, *& had been placed in the temporary house of Representatives the whole Session, was knocked to pieces by the sand stone cutters, & the fragments produced to prove that it could* not be wrought or polished.[91]

Imagine the rage of the sand stone cutters to destroy Latrobe's small sample column and then lie about it! I have to interject an amusing story at this point in the narrative. When I first acquired some Potomac Marble, lacking the tools to do it myself, I searched for someone to cut and polish a few pieces. I eventually found a company in Sterling, Virginia,[92] which makes stone countertops and had the appropriate equipment. But when I showed the piece of Potomac Marble to the head stonecutter, he shook his head and said, "This can't be cut or polished. It will fall apart." So, over two hundred years later, Potomac Marble still scares the bejesus out of stonecutters. It is a stonecutter's nightmare! Eventually, he agreed to do as I asked, and it turned out beautifully as the picture on page 75 demonstrates.

On March 17, 1817, thirteen days after the inauguration, Latrobe appealed to President Monroe to decide in favor of the stone. The president was concerned that it would not support the domed ceiling—a very dangerous situation, indeed, when all of the people's representatives are sitting under that dome! He appointed General Joseph Gardner Swift to investigate along with Colonel George Bomford. Swift, currently the chief of engineers of the U.S. Army, was the first cadet to graduate from West Point in 1802, the superintendent of West Point from 1812 to 1814 and an elected member of the American Philosophical Society.[93] Bomford was from the army's ordnance department and was responsible for building fortifications around Washington.[94]

In their appointment letter, Monroe wrote:

> *Gentlemen: In examining the Capitol in its present state of repair, and the plan for its completion, I find that it is proposed to embellish the Chamber*

*of the House of Representatives with twenty-two columns of marble, and
to erect over the chamber an arch of brick to support the roof, which arch will
rest on the columns; imposing on them a weight of at least 600 tons. The
foundation on which the columns rest is of stone, and, as it is represented,
is supported likewise by arches.* **It is important to me to know
whether these columns, regarding the foundation on
which they rest, and the quality of the marble of which
they are composed, will support such an immense
weight** [author emphasis].[95]

Swift and Bomford rode out to examine the Loudoun County quarries and
then crossed the Potomac to examine those in Montgomery County. They
returned and told the president that Potomac Marble was safe and beautiful.

On March 25, twenty-one days after the inauguration, in the pouring rain,
the president himself along with Swift and Bomford repeated the inspection
tour of Loudoun County, crossed the river at Noland's Ferry, inspected
quarries at Point of Rocks and then traveled downriver near Conrad's Ferry
(now White's Ferry).[96] Convinced, Monroe gave the go-ahead to use Potomac
Marble for the columns of the rebuilt Capitol. To speed up the work, he
appointed Robert Leckie, conductor of the U.S. arsenals, to supervise work
at the quarry and sent Hartnet to Washington to supervise the cutting and
polishing of the stone.[97]

Monroe wrote on April 4, 1817:

*It appearing by a report from Gen'l. Swift…that the marble on the Potomack
from which it has been proposed to obtain the columns intended for the
chamber for the House of Representatives and of the Senate, is of sufficient
solidity to sustain the weight to be placed on them, and likewise that it will
be more adviseable to construct the dome to be erected over the House of
Representatives of wood than of brick, I have on due consideration adopted
their suggestions in both instances.*[98]

Latrobe was not shy about voicing his objections to Monroe's demand for a
wooden dome rather than a brick one. In an earlier letter to Swift and Bomford
on March 31, 1817, he wrote, "A wooden dome is altogether unworthy of the
marble columns" and it "will assuredly perish, and probably by the dry rot.…
But suppose it to last a century, what is a century in the life of nations?"[99]

I find the phrase "what is a century in the life of nations?" to be particularly
compelling. Ever the classicist, Latrobe's thoughts ran to hundreds and

thousands of years. The Parthenon was over two thousand years old and still admired. Why should not the U.S. Capitol follow its lead? Nevertheless, the battle for Potomac Marble had been won, or as Latrobe wrote, "The President soon decided the contest & there are now 100 men, laborers & Stone cutters at work in the Quarry."[100]

Latrobe later wrote to Thomas Jefferson on April 12, 1817:

I have now at the Capitol Nine blocks of Columbian Marble nearly finished for the Columns of the Hall of Representatives. I have never seen anything so beautifully magnificent. Even the most clamorous opposers of their introduction are now silenced. When the columns are in their places, they will be a lasting proof of the firmness of the character of the present President of the U. States; who in order to decide on the merits of the opposition of this Marble, went himself, in the worst weather, to the quarry, and in person gave those orders, which, altho' they did not quell such opposition as could still be made, will ultimately be effectual, & not only render our public buildings rich in nature's magnificence, but make these useless rocks an article of considerable external commerce.[101]

Between his inauguration on March 4, 1817, and one month later, the president of the United States met with a stonemason, organized an expedition of the nation's leading engineers and then did a personal inspection tour of quarries in two states, in the rain, to decide what type of stone should be used for the columns of the Capitol. Could you imagine a modern president doing such a thing today?

In December 1817, in his annual message to Congress, President Monroe clearly explained his motivation and his belief in the importance of Washington becoming a successful capital city:

Most nations have taken an interest and a pride in the improvement and ornament of their metropolis, and none were more conspicuous in that respect than the ancient republics. The policy which dictated the establishment of a permanent residence for the National Government and the spirit in which it was commenced and has been prosecuted show that such improvement was thought worthy the attention of this nation. Its central position, between the northern and southern extremes of our Union, and its approach to the west at the head of a great navigable river which interlocks with the Western waters, prove the wisdom of the councils which established it.[102]

Chapter 6

LATROBE'S POTOMAC MARBLE COLUMNS

*I*f you have toured the Capitol, you have seen the original House Chamber, which today is called the Statuary. While visiting, you probably spent most of your time looking at the statues. This is a shame because, as is clear, particularly after the summer of 2020, statues are ephemeral. What is permanent are Latrobe's Potomac Marble columns. Next time you visit, take some time and look at these beautiful columns, which have stood for over two hundred years while statues have come and gone. (See page 67.)

The Old House Chamber, now called the Statuary, with its Potomac Marble Corinthian columns. *Architect of the Capitol.*

The columns in the Old House Chamber are Corinthian with acanthus leaves carved in their capitals. Acanthus leaves are a traditional classic Greek symbol of immortality and rebirth. You may remember that Latrobe called himself a "bigoted Greek." He loved the Greek classical forms but was not stuck to them. In other parts of the Capitol, he created an "American" Corinthian column using tobacco and corn instead of acanthus leaves. Even though these columns are not carved from Potomac Marble, they are a perfect example of Latrobe's esthetic, so I have included their pictures below and opposite.

As opposed to the Old House Chamber's Corinthian columns, the Old Senate Chamber has Ionic Potomac Marble columns. Ionic columns have scrolls for capitals. Latrobe wrote, "As the Cement which unites the pebbles does not receive quite so high a polish as the pebbles themselves, The Mass acquires a spangled appearance, which adds greatly to the brilliancy of its effect."[103] (See page 69.)

In his 1822 painting *The House of Representatives*, Samuel Morse, a member of the American Philosophical Society and later the inventor of the telegraph, evokes a gorgeous vision of Latrobe's House Chamber at night. Take a look at the painting on page 69.

Latrobe's tobacco leaf capitals located in the Small Senate Rotunda. *Architect of the Capitol.*

Latrobe's corn leaf capitals located in the first-floor vestibule. *Architect of the Capitol.*

Old Senate Chamber with Potomac Marble Ionic columns.

Notice the Potomac Marble columns that hold up the domed ceiling. Between them are the acoustical red curtains that damp out the echoes, and above the Speaker's chair is a large American eagle.

In 1822, there were no electric lights, of course. Lighting at night was provided by a giant whale oil chandelier, as seen in the center of the painting. Later, in the 1830s, the lamp fuel was switched to kerosene and within ten years to natural gas.[104] I have no doubt that the flickering whale oil lamp added to the "spangled appearance" of the columns.

PART II

CHARACTERISTICS OF POTOMAC MARBLE

But the most important characteristic of Potomac Marble is that it is ubiquitous.

—author

Chapter 7

GEOLOGY

About 250 million years ago, during the Triassic period, rivers flowing south from Maryland to Virginia left a fan-shaped deposit of sediment stretching from today's Potomac River to south of Leesburg, Virginia. This sediment hardened over time, becoming a rock later named Potomac Marble. It has had many other names as well: breccia, pebble marble, pudding stone, Loudoun marble, Columbian marble, calico marble, conglomerate and variegated marble.[105]

From a geologist's standpoint, this rock is not actually marble.[106] Marble is metamorphosed limestone, while Potomac Marble is a sedimentary conglomerate of pebbles called clasts by geologists, held together by a limestone calcium carbonate cement matrix. Potomac Marble is often called a *breccia*, which means a conglomerate with angular pebbles, as opposed to *pudding stone*, which is a conglomerate with rounded pebbles. In fact, Latrobe used the word *breccia* most often when discussing this stone, perhaps to differentiate it from marble. The pebbles or clasts vary in size from microscopic to over nine feet. Some pebble! An analysis of pebble counts, "from 29 selected locations…show 94% limestone and dolomitic limestone, 2% dolomite, 1% greenstone, 2% quartzite and metamorphosed feldspathic sandstone, and 1% slate, schist, chert, and siltstone."[107]

One of the fascinating facts about Potomac Marble is derived from its angular pebbles. Their angularity suggests that they were deposited by the rivers so quickly that the water did not have a chance to smooth their edges. Also, in most cases the clasts are pointing in different directions, which geologists call unsorted, also implying limited action by water. (See page 74.)

Geologist Joseph K. Roberts found two basic varieties of Potomac Marble based on color. Near Leesburg, he found samples with a white matrix and elsewhere a more reddish matrix because of the presence of ferric oxide.[108] This is somewhat borne out by my research; the only white stone I found was in Leesburg at the old Leesburg Limestone Company site discussed in chapter 12.

To become actual marble, the Potomac Marble conglomerate would have to be subjected to extreme heat and pressure—that is, metamorphosed. There *are* deposits of actual marble in Loudoun County. One geologist suggests it was formed when an igneous intrusion into the Potomac Marble deposits metamorphosized the Potomac Marble into marble.[109] That igneous intrusion is now quarried as diabase for road beds and gravel at the Luck Stone Quarry just east of Leesburg.

Latrobe was aware of the Loudoun County marble as early as April 1800, when he proposed a pyramid-shaped memorial to George Washington, who had died four months earlier. The walls would be built from local granite and

The entrance to the Luck Stone diabase quarry east of Leesburg.

The Luck Stone diabase quarry is over three hundred feet deep, and each tier is a road wide enough for dump trucks.

"the Columns of white marble, either from Pennsa. or from the County of Loudoun in Virginia."[110] Later he wrote, "We have in America marble very superior in texture to that of Carrara in Italy which is the kind always used for statues....The difficulty here is that our quarries are scarcely opened....I have found as good as any in the world in Loudoun County Virga."[111] (See page 71.)

The marble from Loudoun County is quite lovely,[112] but Potomac Marble is even lovelier. On page 72, compare the picture of marble samples to the Potomac Marble samples taken from various quarries in Loudoun and Montgomery Counties and cut and polished by my friend Jim Kostka. Notice the pebbles of various shapes, sizes and colors all held together by a calcium carbonate matrix.

Covering 18 square miles of Loudoun County with a maximum width of 1.5 miles, Potomac Marble deposits stretch from the Maryland side of the Potomac to south of Leesburg, Virginia. For the geologists, the matrix measures 4 on the Mohs Hardness Scale, where 10 is diamond and 1 is talc.[113]

Above: A Potomac Marble outcrop at Ida Lee Park, Leesburg.

Left: A Potomac Marble outcrop in Leesburg with an unusually large clast.

Opposite, top: Potomac Marble boulders making a bold statement in a garden at Ida Lee Park in Leesburg.

Opposite, bottom: Potomac Marble boulders at the old hospital grounds in Leesburg.

Two huge Potomac Marble boulders on the lawn of a Leesburg apartment complex.

A Potomac Marble boulder at a Leesburg carwash.

A gardener using Potomac Marble boulders dug out of her backyard to line her flower bed.

A road lined with Potomac Marble boulders dug up while building Smart's Mill Middle School in Leesburg.

Potomac Marble outcrops at Rockcroft Farm in Lucketts, Virginia.

But the most important characteristic of Potomac Marble is that it is ubiquitous. Once called by farmers "an incumbrance to agriculture,"[114] its omnipresence helps explain the great fertility of Loudoun County soil and the presence of limekilns throughout the area. Indeed, a well dug as deep as 360 feet in Leesburg did not penetrate the rock,[115] and the deposit is thought to be as deep as 3,510 feet.[116]

Chapter 8

SINKHOLES

*A*nother characteristic of Potomac Marble is its solubility. As water seeps through the bedrock, it creates sinkholes or karsts. To alleviate this problem, Loudoun County has created a Limestone Overlay District, which overlays the area of Potomac Marble, excluding Leesburg, which is outside of its jurisdiction. Developers building in this district are required to X-ray the ground beneath to make sure they are not building on a karst.

On the following page is Loudoun County's sinkhole map, where every black dot represents a known sinkhole as of 2017. As you can see, sinkholes (karsts) are quite common.

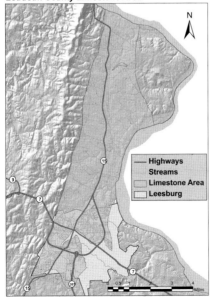

The Loudoun County limestone area excluding Leesburg. *Loudoun County.*

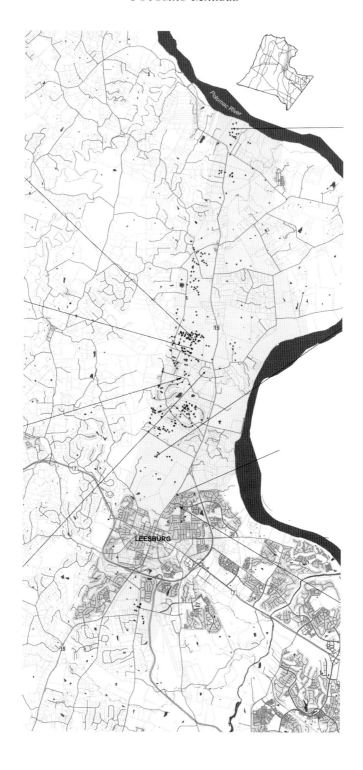

GOVERNMENT

Crews work to clear up a sinkhole problem at the construction site for the Pennington Parking Lot in downtown Leesburg.   Courtesy Photo/Loudoun County

Supervisors cough up $3.5M for sinkhole fix

BY SYDNEY KASHIWAGI
skashiwagi@loudountimes.com

Loudoun County supervisors threw money down a hole Tuesday night.

After the county discovered two 70-80-foot sinkholes earlier this summer under North Street's Pennington Parking Lot being constructed in downtown Leesburg, the board signed off Tuesday on $3.5 million to fix the problem despite little assurances from engineers that the sinkholes would go away for good and not affect neighboring properties.

Additional work on the sinkholes will add a 150-day delay to the overall project schedule. The project is now scheduled for completion in November 2018.

For years, Leesburg residents and local politicians have resisted the size and scope of the Pennington lot, which is tied to the long-awaited courthouse expansion — a project that cannot be constructed until the parking structure is built.

"Is anything we do to remediate this situation going to increase the likelihood that any sinkholes may develop under [nearby residents'] properties?" asked Supervisor Kristen Umstattd (D-Leesburg).

Umstattd also pressed the county's third party geotechnical engineers on whether capping the sinkhole area would push water away from it and instead toward surrounding properties, cause flooding or even more sinkholes in nearby residents' properties.

But all of her questions were met with a slew of unknowns.

"Sinkholes are unpredictable," Nicholas Meloy, a senior project engineer with the engineering firm ECS, responded, explaining that sinkholes develop from voids in the rock underground due to its natural weathering and, therefore, cannot be predicted.

To fix the problem, engineers have recommended cap grouting and compaction grouting at the site and in a 60-foot diameter surrounding the sinkhole. Additionally, they have recommended more cap grouting under additional pile caps that were deemed at risk, according to the county.

Cap grouting is a process by which a thick grout is injected to build a concrete cap over a distressed area. The technique prevents additional soil loss into the sinkhole. However, Tennessee-based Rembco Geotechnical Contractors, Inc. says cap grouting by itself "does not return the site to a useable condition."

"The remediation efforts that are going on are stopping at the rock surface, so we don't believe that the remediation efforts pose a significant increase in risk for surrounding properties," Meloy said.

Meloy said it was "extremely difficult to predict" what would happen to the direction of the water after the cap and grouting process. After they cap the bedrock of the area, he said the water would "find the path of least resistance" afterwards.

Meloy also said he did not anticipate groundwater would cause flooding in nearby properties because the rock was deep at some places he did not think it would happen. But again, he stressed he did not know for certain where the groundwater would travel and whether other sinkholes would occur in the area.

Altogether, the county says it needs $500,000 for sinkhole remediation; nearly $3 million for cap grouting at "at-risk" pile caps; $62,315 for improvements to slab-on-grade; and $9,985 for improvements to the garage entry way.

All of the additional sinkhole improvements costs except the $3 million cap grouting work have either already been approved or will later be approved under the county's purchasing agent award.

Department of Transportation and Capital Infrastructure Director Joe Kroboth told supervisors the county likely created the sinkhole when they drilled the piles that support the lot.

Supervisors were taken aback when ECS said that after conducting tests on the structure, they knew it was expected to be on a bedrock that was known for "harsh activity and potential for sinkholes."

Kroboth said his department budgeted for potential setbacks, but simply "did not expect the magnitude of the change that's before us."

Kroboth admitted his department would ask for more money in the fiscal 2019 Capital Improvement Program budget.

Oth   visors wondered if more sinkhol   develop under the area of the future courthouse construction.

Kroboth explained the Pennington lot had a different structural design than the courts building. He said the courthouse would sit on a structural slab set on piles,

while the Pennington Parking Lot was not set on piles, but the concrete slabs on the first floor were laying on ground.

"We're confident that the courts design is adequate. We are going to go back and knowing the information that we have, re-evaluate the design and possibly increase the pile size so that if a large area opened up, it could structurally support the building," Kroboth said.

But some were still wary of the engineer's and staff's assurances and torn on approving additional funds.

"I'm really afraid that we're getting ourselves into an old fashion boondoggle as far as throwing our money down a hole, literally and figuratively, in this case," said Supervisor Ron Meyer (R-Broad Run).

Meyer and other supervisors asked if other locations could be considered to move the lot or if they could go back and lower the lot of three levels to avoid the problem.

But staff said lowering the lot would not fix the problem and moving it would cost significantly more.

"This is one of the more unsettling staff reports I've heard in a long time," Chairwoman Phyllis Randall (D-At Large) said. "It feels like half of Loudoun County is about to fall into a sinkhole because they're unpredictable."

The board ultimately voted 7-2, with Supervisors Meyer and Umstattd opposed, to award Howard Shockey & Sons, the project's contractor, $2,973,520 million more to fix the sinkholes, bringing the total of its contract for the parking lot from $12.7 million $15.9 million.

Opposite: A map of karsts (sinkholes) in Loudoun County. *Courtesy of the Office of Mapping and Geographic Information, Loudoun County, Virginia.*

Above: *Loudoun Times Mirror*, September 6, 2017, reports on two sinkholes delaying construction of a Leesburg town parking lot. The town spent over $3.5 million for repairs. *Courtesy of the* Loudoun Times Mirror.

Even with all these precautions, sinkholes present a constant problem. A recent example occurred on July 8, 2021, when a sinkhole suddenly appeared along Route 15, the main north–south route between Leesburg, Virginia, and Frederick, Maryland, temporarily shutting down the road.

A few years earlier, on September 6, 2017, two sinkholes, seventy to eighty feet deep, were discovered during the construction of a county parking garage on North Street in downtown Leesburg. Eventually, it cost $3.5 million to fix the problem and held up construction for over five months.

Chapter 9

CAVERNS

*I*n addition to sinkholes, Loudoun County has multiple underwater caverns. One of the more well known is under Carlheim Manor in Leesburg. Formerly known as Paxton, this estate is now part of the Arc of Loudoun, a private school. I visited in October 2018, and the school's director, Lisa Kimball, was kind enough to allow me to take photographs. Loudoun historian Eugene Scheel writes:

> *The limestone region's most famous caves are underneath Carlheim....In 1872, as Carlheim neared completion, a builder James L. Norris wrote owner Charles Paxton, informing him that there were three large caverns at the bottom of an 80-foot well. In the letter, Norris's workman described the caverns as a "rather frightful looking place with an air of mystery and dread which he cannot shake off."*[117]

My first stop was that "80-foot well," which allowed access to the "frightful looking place." Alas, it is now sealed in concrete, which is prudent given the fact that the estate has been an orphanage, a daycare center and now a school.

The school's facility director, Matt Smith, offered to show me another entrance to the cavern that was inside the manor house. I followed him into the old building, and he led me to the basement stairs. Despite the oft-quoted admonition, "Don't go into the basement," I followed Smith to the lower level, where it was dark, damp and quite spooky. The path continued

Opposite, top: Beneath Carlheim Mansion in Leesburg is a large underground cavern and lake.

Opposite, bottom: This is the original entrance to the cavern at Carlheim Mansion, now sealed for safety.

Above: The "Well of Lost Souls" at Carlheim Mansion provided access to the cavern in the past but is now a favorite Halloween display.

circuitously between pipes and boilers until we, at last, arrived at the "Well of Lost Souls."

Draped with skeletons and other old bones, the Well of Lost Souls is one of the highlights of Arc of Loudoun's Shocktober fundraising event. It is a real well, now filled in but in the past a ready water supply.

Mr. Smith told me that the school still receives a monthly check for water use from the Town of Leesburg. That seemed quite odd because Leesburg's water supply is drawn from the seemingly unlimited Potomac River. Always curious, I called Russell Chambers, Leesburg's utility plant manager, and he confirmed that Leesburg maintains a link to this ancient cavern's reservoir as a backup water supply.

Benjamin Latrobe, by
George B. Mathews.
Architect of the Capitol.

Richard Chenoweth's re-creation of the Capitol in 1812. The building on the left housed
the Senate, Library of Congress and the Supreme Court. On the right was the House of
Representatives. *Courtesy of Richard Chenoweth.*

Above: Richard Chenoweth's re-creation of Jefferson's and Latrobe's House of Representatives in 1812, "the most beautiful room in the world." *Courtesy of Richard Chenoweth.*

Right: Charles Willson Peale, *The Artist in His Museum*, 1822. Peale was Latrobe's good friend and a fellow member of the American Philosophical Society. *Oil on canvas framed: 116x92x5 in. (294.64x233.68x12.7 cm.); 103¾x79 7/8 in. (263.525x202.8825 cm.). Courtesy of the Pennsylvania Academy of the Fine Arts, Philadelphia. Gift of Mrs. Sarah Harrison (The Joseph Harrison, Jr. Collection), 1878.1.2.*

British Burn the Capitol, 1814, by Allyn Cox. The painting can be found at the Capitol in the corridor of the House wing on the first floor. *Architect of the Capitol.*

The Old House Chamber, now called the Statuary, as it looks today. *Architect of the Capitol.*

Close-up of Potomac Marble columns and Corinthian capitals in the old House Chamber.

Close-up of the Potomac Marble composing the columns in the Old House Chamber.

Old Senate Chamber with its Ionic columns as it appears today. *Architect of the Capitol.*

The House of Representatives, Samuel F.B. Morse, 1822. This is Latrobe's chamber in all its beauty. *National Gallery, Washington, D.C.*

Old Aquia sandstone quarry near Government Island, Stafford County, Virginia.

Sample of sandstone from the Aquia Creek Quarry on Government Island.

The Capitol crypt where George Washington was to be buried. The columns are Aquia Creek sandstone.

Marble from Loudoun County on the left and in the center, cut and polished by the author. Latrobe proposed a monument to George Washington be built from Loudoun County marble. On the right is Carrara Italian marble.

Potomac Marble samples from Loudoun and Montgomery Counties cut and polished by the author.

Potomac Marble samples cut and polished by James Kostka of Leesburg, Virginia, showing the stone's variety in color and pattern.

Typically, construction sites in the Loudoun limestone area turn up Potomac Marble boulders, such as shown here. In this case, it was during the construction of a new tennis court in Ida Lees Park, Leesburg.

This sinkhole on a farm in Lucketts, Virginia, is a convenient place to throw downed trees and other detritus. Look closely and you will see Potomac Marble foundation stones from a torn-down building.

Close-up of a Potomac Marble outcrop in Ida Lee Park in Leesburg, Virginia, showing the matrix, clasts and various colors. Notice how the clasts are angular and unsorted.

Potomac Marble boulder from Olde Izaak Walton Park Quarry in Leesburg.

Lovely picture of a palm warbler sitting on an outcrop of Potomac Marble at Olde Izaak Walton Park in Leesburg. *Michael Meyers.*

Gorgeous polished samples of Potomac Marble from Olde Izaak Walton Quarry in Leesburg, cut by Erin's Marble and Granite of Sterling, Virginia, and polished by the author.

Potomac Marble sample, cut and polished by the author, from the Leesburg Limestone Company quarry in Leesburg. Its "white" color disqualifies it from being the source of the Old House Chamber columns.

Remains of the kilns at the Leesburg Limestone Company quarry in Leesburg. These are easily accessible by way of the W&OD bike path at Depot Street.

Above: Billowing Potomac Marble outcrops at Camp Kanawha near Point of Rocks, Maryland.

Left: Members of an "expedition" to the Latrobe quarry scramble up the steep hill toward its entrance in January 2021. Notice the C&O Canal at the bottom of the steep hill.

The author at Latrobe's quarry. Directly behind him is the largest remaining wall of the Potomac Marble outcrop. Above and to the left is red sandstone. *Jon Wolz.*

Inside the Latrobe quarry overlooking the Potomac River and the C&O Canal.

The man in the red jacket is standing in Latrobe's quarry, demonstrating how difficult it is to see it from the towpath, even in winter.

The Seneca Bypass Canal pictured here was one of many sluices and bypasses built by George Washington's Potomac Company. This one bypassed Seneca Falls.

Potomac Marble jewelry box created by Brian D. Cole of Orrtanna, Pennsylvania.

Potomac Marble orb created by James Kostka of Leesburg, Virginia. Kostka used Potomac Marble found near Latrobe's quarry.

PART III

THE SEARCH FOR THE QUARRIES

The quarries are situated in Loudoun County, Virginia and Montgomery County, Maryland.

—Benjamin Latrobe, November 28, 1816

Chapter 10

BACKGROUND

As my interest in Potomac Marble began with the supposition that the current Olde Izaak Walton Park in Leesburg was one of the quarry sources for Latrobe, I began to search in earnest for proof. Latrobe wrote in multiple documents that "the quarries are situated in Loudoun County, Virginia and Montgomery County, Maryland,"[118] never seemingly being more specific. The search became quite frustrating because the specific locations are never revealed by either his contemporaries or those who write about them. The mystery starts quite early. For example, Samuel Lane, the commissioner of public buildings, lists a disbursement dated May 21, 1816, for $16.00 for "Hack hire to marble quarries" and another paid to Latrobe for $161.27 for "Expenses exploring marble quarries."[119] Which marble quarries? Who owns them? Where are they?

Latrobe's biographer Talbot Hamlin, in his six-hundred-page work, makes no attempt to identify quarry locations and only repeats a story told by Latrobe's son about the discovery of the marble on the Loudoun estate of Samuel Clapham.[120] He implies that the quarries were on this estate, but there is no other proof of this, and much of the rest of the story is apocryphal.[121]

Other historians wrote that the marble came from the "banks of the Potomac River, just above Conrad's Ferry";[122] "both sides of the Potomac River in Loudoun County, Virginia and Montgomery County Maryland";[123] and "in Loudoun County Virginia."[124]

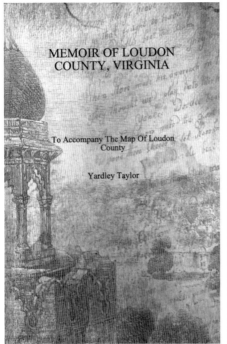
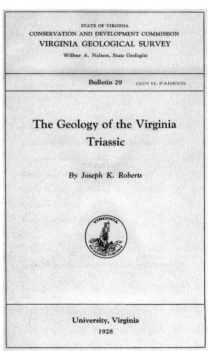

Left: Yardley Taylor's 1858 book accompanied the first comprehensive map of Loudoun County but offers no clues to the location of Latrobe's quarry.

Right: Geologist Joseph Roberts in this 1928 book also offers no clues to the location of Latrobe's quarry.

Cartographers are not any clearer. For example, a much-quoted early Loudoun cartographer, Yardley Taylor, while discussing Potomac Marble in his 1858 *Memoir of Loudoun County*, says, "This rock was used for the pillars in the Capitol at Washington, and may be seen in the Representatives Hall and Senate Chamber."[125] Taylor never identifies a Loudoun quarry location even on his 1853 map, which is the first detailed map of Loudoun County and can be seen at the Balch Library in Leesburg.

Geologists are no exception. The 1898 Maryland Geological Survey reports, "There is some doubt as to the exact location of the particular source of these blocks used in the capitol."[126] Joseph K. Roberts writes in his 1928 book, the *Geology of the Triassic*:

> *The rock was first noted by B.H. Latrobe who selected it for columns in the National capitol. It would seem from Latrobe's account that the quarries*

from which the stone was taken were located in Loudoun County, Virginia and in Montgomery County, Maryland.[127]

Oh no! There is that phrase again: "Located in Loudoun County, Virginia and Montgomery County, Maryland."

Government publications do not provide much more help. In a pamphlet published in 1975 by the U.S. Department of Interior, *Building Stones of Our Nation's Capital*, it is written, "Until the Chesapeake and Ohio Canal was finished, the huge blocks were brought overland from quarries near Point of Rocks, Maryland, 46 miles west of Washington."[128] Interestingly, when that pamphlet was republished in 1998, it was ten pages smaller and says only that Potomac Marble came from "various localities."[129]

There is, on the Chesapeake and Ohio Canal towpath, a Marble Quarry Campsite at milepost 38.2. On the C&O Canal Trust web page, it is described as follows:

According to old maps, before the C&O Canal was built, there was a "Marble Quarry" running along the Maryland side of the river for over a mile. The stone that was quarried here was known as "Potomac marble," which wasn't a solid substance, but rather was composed of angular pebbles held together by a limestone matrix. Benjamin Latrobe discovered Potomac Marble with its varied and rich colors and made the decision to include it in the Capitol buildings he was designing.[130]

I have found no evidence of a quarry near this campsite.

This leads us to ask, "Doesn't there exist at least one two-hundred-year-old hole in the ground that we can prove was a source of the Potomac Marble for the columns in the Capitol?"

Chapter 11

OLDE IZAAK WALTON PARK

*E*minent Loudoun historian and mapmaker Eugene Scheel writes, "In 1976 I called the Capitol historian, and he told me that the stone came from quarries in Leesburg and by the Potomac in Maryland." Scheel suggests two locations in Loudoun that may have been sources of Potomac Marble for Latrobe: Olde Izaak Walton Park and the Leesburg Limestone Quarry, both within the town limits of Leesburg.[131]

Olde Izaak Walton Park is the former location of the Loudoun County Chapter of the Izaak Walton League of America (LCC-IWLA), one of the country's oldest conservation organizations. As the town of Leesburg grew in the twentieth century, it became untenable to have shooting ranges and other amenities offered by the League within town borders. In the 1960s, therefore, the League moved its operations southwest of town to its present eighty-eight-acre location, and the original property eventually became the town park it is now.

Scheel hypothesizes that the park's pond is the location of the original quarry. Using a device attached to a fishing rod, I surveyed the depth of the pond. In no place was it more than seven feet deep, too shallow for a quarry.[132]

I also have in my possession snapshots dated July 1955. They were sent by the son of an original member of the LCC-IWLA, Tom Caviness. In his accompanying letter, Caviness says that snapshots show the pond being dug at that date.[133] The pond is not the quarry, but there *is* a quarry on this site. Walk about five hundred feet west of the pond, past the parking lot, and you will be overlooking the quarry, hidden by overgrowth and poison ivy vines.

Left: The entrance to Olde Izaak Walton Park, rumored to be the source of Latrobe's Potomac Marble columns.

Below: The pond at Olde Izaak Walton Park, rumored to be Latrobe's quarry.

Samples from this old quarry reveal a very beautiful Potomac Marble (see page 75). Its quality is certainly good enough to have been used in the Capitol, but there are no records that I could find to actually connect it to the Capitol rebuild. I have also not found any records yet that tell me the age of this quarry. All we have so far is an oral tradition.

A picture from July 1955 showing the excavation of the Olde Izaak Walton Pond, proving it wasn't a quarry. *Courtesy of Tom Caviness.*

The actual quarry at Olde Izaak Walton Park, with my friend Jim Kostka providing the size context.

Scheel also writes, "From 1793 to 1817, when the U.S. Capitol was built and then rebuilt after the British burned it in 1814, the Potomac Marble was delivered the 40 miles, then cut, polished and put in place."[134] This cannot be true because Potomac Marble was not used at all in the Capitol until 1817.

My guess is that as lime is an extremely important product for both agriculture and construction, it may very well be that Potomac Marble from this quarry traveled to Washington, but it traveled there in powdered form after being processed by a limekiln. In Washington, it may have been used in manufacturing the cement critical to every construction project and, in that sense, may have helped build the Capital City and aided in the rebuild of the Capitol after the fire of 1814.

Chapter 12

LEESBURG LIMESTONE COMPANY

*A*s I wrote in the beginning of the previous section, historian Scheel suggested two quarries in Leesburg as a source of the columns. Here we will deal with Leesburg Limestone Company quarry. This quarry is a few blocks away from downtown Leesburg on Depot Street. When I first moved to Leesburg in 1985, it was filled with water, and I was told that it was a tradition for graduates of Loudoun County High School to take a graduation swim. In the 1990s, it was filled in with the intention of selling the land for development. However, because of the low quality of the landfill used, the owners have not been able to get a permit to build, and it is now rented to car dealers as a parking lot.[135]

Geologist Joseph Roberts writes, "The quarry in 1920 was rectangular in opening, 350 x 300 feet at the surface, 285 feet at bottom, and the average depth was approximately 106 feet....The initial output was about 200 bushels as compared with 125,000 in 1919."[136] It was also the major employer of African Americans in the area,[137] and you can still find locals who remember their grandfathers talking about working in the quarry.

It was difficult to get samples of the Potomac Marble from this quarry given that it is now a parking lot. We were fortunate, though, to locate some groundhog burrows on the property. The groundhogs had kicked out nice-size samples of the marble for our use. As you can see on page 76, the polished marble is beautiful, but the color is mostly white, missing the bold reds and browns of the other quarries (and the columns) caused by an infusion of ferric oxide. We know that this quarry operated from 1868 until

A. View of the Leesburg Lime Company's quarry operating in the Border Conglomerate (limestone phase) on the east side of Leesburg, Loudoun County.

Photograph of the Leesburg Limestone Company quarry in 1928. *Joseph K. Roberts, "The Geology of the Virginia Triassic."*

A view of the Leesburg Limestone Company quarry today. It has been filled in and is used as a parking lot for car dealers.

Above: Remains of a rail car loading station at the Leesburg Limestone Company quarry.

Opposite: A stone wall built from Potomac Marble quarried from the Leesburg Limestone Company quarry.

1945,[138] but as with the Olde Izaak Walton Park quarry, I have located no evidence except oral history that it was ever used as more than a limestone quarry producing lime for agriculture and construction.

Chapter 13

FINALLY, SUCCESS!

In the April 8, 1817 issue of the *Genius of Liberty*, a local Leesburg, Virginia paper, appeared the following advertisement:[139]

Wanted Immediately.
At the Marble Quarry, Montgomery County, Maryland, on the Potomac,
ONE HUNDRED STRONG, HEALTHY,
Laboring Men
To whom liberal wages will be given, and for strong and healthy negro men
Ninety Dollars *from the first of April until the first of January next; or in proportion for such time as they shall remain at the Quarry.*
By order of the President of the U. States.
SAMUEL LANE, Commissioner of the public buildings
APPLY TO
John Nelson, esq. Frederick Town,
John Littlejohn, esq Leesburg,
John Hartnett at the Quarry,
Joshua Shelton, near Conrad's ferry,
Major Noland, at Aldie (Loudoun)
Samuel Clapham, esq
The printer of the paper, Alexandria
And the Commissioner of the public buildings at Washington
March 28th

THE GENIUS OF LIBERTY.

PRINTED BY C. R. SAUNDERS, (FOR SAMUEL B. T. CALDWELL,) LEESBURG, Va. AT TWO DOLLS. PER ANNUM—IN ADVANCE.

VOL. I.]   TUESDAY, APRIL 8, 1817.   [No. 13

An advertisement in *The Genius of Liberty* on April 8, 1817, seeking workers for Latrobe's quarry. *Courtesy of the Library of Virginia.*

All of the ad's signers were important in their communities, and many of them had a direct relationship to Latrobe and the rebuilding effort in the Capital. For example, according to Eugene Scheel, John Littlejohn was a Methodist minister and sheriff in Leesburg and was part of the chain that preserved the Constitution and other important state papers that were hurriedly removed from Washington for safekeeping immediately before the burning in the summer of 1814.[140]

"John Hartnett at the quarry" was an experienced marble mason who was placed in charge of shaping the Potomac Marble columns when they arrived in Washington. According to an article in the *National Intelligencer* of January 24, 1817, in June 1816, Commissioner Samuel Lane contracted with Hartnet, "an experienced marble mason, for all the columns and pilasters of the House of Rep."[141]

Most important, though, is Samuel Clapham. The Clapham family was active in Loudoun County for generations, involved in farming, quarrying and canals. Their estate house, named Chestnut Hill, still stands just west of Route 15 in northern Loudoun County. It was Samuel Clapham who owned the land leased by the U.S. government in 1817 for Latrobe's Potomac Marble quarry. In an August 8, 1815 letter to the commissioners of public buildings, Latrobe identifies Clapham:

There is on the S. East of the Catocktin Mountain a very large extent of country, which abounds in immense Rocks of Marble, or Limestone Breccia, *that is of a Stone consisting of fragments of ancient Rocks bound together by calcareous cement, and thus becoming one solid and uniform (homogeneous) Mass of Marble. This Range of Rocks I have traced from James River to the Delaware, but it appears nowhere of a more beautiful kind then on the Patowmac. A specimen will be submitted to you as soon as I can get it polished.*

The largest Mass of this Kind of Rock is situated on the Maryland side of the Patowmac on land the property of Samuel Clapham, Esqr. It overhangs the River, and would furnish without any land carriage all the Columns of the Capitol of one block each *if required, and of beauty not exceeded in any modern or ancient building.*[142]

In February 1816, the commissioners contracted with Samuel Clapham to quarry the marble.[143] On March 14, 1816, Latrobe sketched the outcrop and titled the piece "Breccia Marble Rock opposite Clapham Island."[144] Clapham Island, now called Mason Island, is about 1.5 miles long and

Samuel Clapham's eighteenth-century mansion, Chestnut Hill, in northern Loudoun County off Route 15. Clapham sold his land along the Potomac River to the government, and it became the Latrobe quarry.

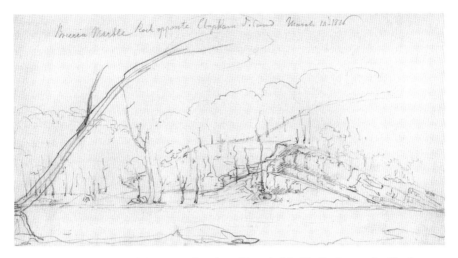

Latrobe's 1816 drawing of the quarry location: "Breccia Marble Rock opposite Clapham Island." The quarry was a massive outcrop of Potomac Marble reaching out into the Potomac River. *Courtesy of the Maryland Center for History and Culture.*

is divided into upper and lower sections by a cut through the island. The Marble Quarry campsite, mentioned previously, is directly across from the cut between the two sections.

All of this evidence, and more, pointed to the location of a quarry in a 1.5-mile stretch along the Maryland shore of the Potomac River across from Mason Island. Conveniently, this is now the C&O Canal National Park, and the old canal towpath is well maintained alongside the old canal prism, which is dry in many places. A search by your author in the autumn of 2018 failed to find the quarry.

Then, a breakthrough!

In 2018, Mary Oehrlein, the historic preservation officer at the Capitol (now retired), sent to me a memorandum dated January 1965 and written by Owen H. Ramsburg, an engineer employed by the Office of the Architect of the Capitol (AOC). It was addressed to Mario E. Campioli, the assistant architect of the Capitol and the man in charge of restoration of the old Senate Chamber. It reads, "This investigation and report was made in order to find similar marble to be used in the restoration of the Old Senate Chamber."[145]

In an attempt to locate "similar marble," Ramsburg consulted many of the same sources I had used, only to find the same ambiguous results. At first, thinking that the Point of Rocks area in Maryland was the probable location of the original quarry, Ramsburg made multiple visits to the area, in particular visiting Camp Kanawha, a private club that still exists near Point

1

January, 1965

Memorandum

To: Mario E. Campioli

From: Owen H. Ramsburg

Subject: Report on Potomac Marble

Attached is a report on the Potomac Marble used for the columns
in the Old House and Senate Chambers and the Colonnade outside the
entrance to the Old Senate Chamber, including visits to the site
of the stratum of marble by Mr. Mario E. Campioli, Mr. Frank X. Kuhn
and the writer.

OHR

Above: January 1965 memorandum from Owen H. Ramsburg to Mario E. Campioli on the location of Latrobe's quarry. *Courtesy of the Architect of the Capitol, Records, Office of the Curator, Capitol Stone files, 1965.*

Opposite, top: The entrance to Camp Kanawha near Point of Rocks, Maryland.

Opposite, bottom: Camp Kanawha's Potomac Marble outcrops near Point of Rocks.

of Rocks.[146] Potomac Marble samples were taken at the camp and along the nearby Baltimore and Ohio Railroad tracks. In all, three visits were made to this area between October and December 1964 by Ramsburg and Frank X. Kuhn, a stone expert employed by the AOC. The men remained unsatisfied that the source of the marble columns was there.

The investigation received critical evidence when Benjamin Latrobe's article in the *National Intelligencer* from January 24, 1817, was located by Ramsburg. In this article, Latrobe writes:

> *The Potomac, breaking through the Cotecktin mountain, crosses the Breccia until it meets the Monocasy under the S.E. side of the valley; it then suddenly turns to the S.W. and again enters the Breccia, leaving a large mass on the Maryland side (the east side) of the river, by far the highest part of this irregular compound. It immediately however turns to the S.E. and at Conrad's Ferry leaves the Breccia finally. On this high mass in Maryland, in which the quarry is opened.*[147]

Further search on this "high mass in Maryland" above White's Ferry revealed that the land was broken up roughly into two bluffs with a deep ravine between them. A thorough search was made of the area, but to no avail. Finally, National Park Service rangers were mobilized in January 1965, and an expedition was organized. On February 1, 1965, Chief Ranger Bell of the National Park Service announced they had located the quarry 2.2 miles upriver from White's Ferry.

It took two attempts on my part to find Latrobe's quarry despite the specific instructions of the Ramsburg report.[148] The quarry is impossible to see from the towpath when there are leaves on the trees and difficult when there are none (see page 79). Using an accurate GPS device, I walked upriver on the towpath from White's Ferry. The river is always on the left, and in a mile or so the farmland on the right gives way to a growing stone ridge. The occasional drill marks in the ridge are from the later C&O Canal construction and are not relevant to our search. The quarry is located at the top of this ridge at exactly 2.2 miles. Fortunately, the canal is shallow in this area and can be easily crossed, but if it has rained recently, wading boots are recommended. Climb the ridge and enter the quarry. Over fifty years later, it is exactly as described in the report by Ramsburg in 1965:

> *Some of the sides of the quarry show drill marks as do one or more blocks laying loose in the bottom of the quarry. The south wall or side of the pit*

A map showing the location of the Latrobe quarry. *Google Earth Pro.*

The author in front of the largest remaining wall in Latrobe's quarry. *Jon Wolz.*

The view from Latrobe's quarry of the C&O Canal, towpath and the Potomac River. Notice the Potomac Marble boulder in the picture's foreground.

The author and historian Jon Wolz examining quarried Potomac Marble boulders on the Potomac River shore during a period of low water. *Doug Zveare*.

Latrobe's quarry is located at Mile Post 38 on the C&O Canal towpath. The Potomac River is in the background.

is practically solid Potomac marble. The east wall has two to eight feet or more thick seams of the red sandstone of the Newark formation between which are seams of Potomac Marble. On the north side, the bottom of the pit, in general, meets the natural slope of the bluff and at the west side the floor of the pit drops off abruptly to the canal below.[149]

Interestingly, during a search along the water's edge in the immediate area of the quarry, some marble blocks were found half-buried in the mud.[150] Was this the result of a careless boatman loading the cargo back in 1817 or simply debris scattered from the quarry over a two-hundred-year period? Further investigation is needed.

Is there a "hole in the ground" we can identify as the source of the beautiful columns in the Old House and Senate Chambers? Now, at last, we can answer, "Yes, there is!" It is located 2.2 miles upriver from White's Ferry on the C&O Canal towpath, and its coordinates are 39.177192, -77.4960702. Fortuitously, as my friend, historian and journalist John Wolz, pointed out, this is exactly at the clearly marked Mile Post 38 on the C&O Canal towpath.[151]

Chapter 14

CONFIRMATION BY CONTEMPORARY SOURCES

*I*n subsequent investigations aided by Jon Wolz, contemporary sources confirmed this quarry as *the* quarry used by Latrobe. At the suggestion of canal historian Karen Gray, Wolz requested and received from the ever-helpful librarians at the National Archives II a box containing two journals. The first was the Geddes & Roberts Survey & Level Book from March 1828, a mere ten years after the quarry was active. This survey was

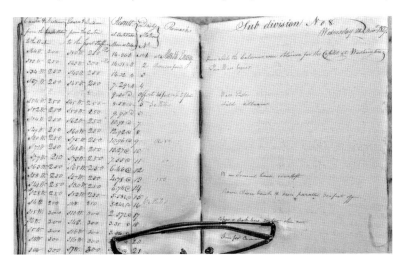

A page from the Geddes & Roberts Survey & Level Book dated November 28, 1828, in which is written, "at Marble quarry…from which the columns were obtained for the Capitol at Washington."

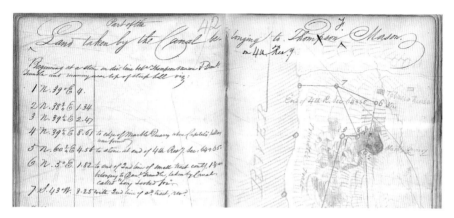

A notebook probably compiled beginning in January 1830 in which it is written, "to edge of Marble Quarry where Capitol's columns were found ["or from"—author]." On the right side is a hand-drawn map labeled "Marble Quarry."

done in preparation for the construction of the C&O Canal. Surveyor Geddes on November 28, 1828, wrote in the notebook, "Marble Quarry," and continued, "From which the columns were obtained for the Capitol at Washington."[152]

The second notebook, which is unsigned, has an entry on page 42, "approaching marble quarry," and then a map and drawing of the quarry. Its location is exactly where it should be based on our other evidence.[153]

PART IV

ROCK BECOMES STONE

I have never seen anything so beautifully magnificent.

—*Benjamin Latrobe, August 12, 1817*

Chapter 15

GEOLOGIC INTRODUCTION

*I*n the introduction to this book, I discussed the distinction between a rock and a stone. A stone is simply a rock that we have made useful or valuable. In this chapter, I will discuss the methods and tools used in the early nineteenth century to turn rock to stone, emphasizing two rocks important to our story: Aquia Creek sandstone and Potomac Marble.

It will be helpful to the reader if we review some basic eighth-grade earth science. You may remember that there are three types of rock:

- Igneous rock is molten rock, or magma, from the bowels of the earth. When it comes to the surface in a volcano, it is called lava.
  - An example of igneous rock is the diabase or trap stone quarried at the Luck Stone Quarry east of Leesburg, Virginia.
  - Another example is the granite countertop in your kitchen.
- Sedimentary rock is the result of sand or pebbles (sediment) deposited usually by water and then solidified into a rock chemically or by pressure and heat.
  - Sandstone is a sedimentary rock composed, usually, of quartz grains held together by a silica matrix.
  - Limestone is also sedimentary, but its sediment is held together by a calcium carbonate matrix.
  - Conglomerate is a sedimentary rock with clasts (pebbles). If the pebbles are angular, it is called a breccia; otherwise, it is known as a pudding stone.

- Metamorphic rocks are formed by subjecting rock to pressure and heat.
  - Marble, for example such as that from the Carrara quarries in Italy, is created when limestone is metamorphosized.
  - When sandstone is metamorphosized, it becomes quartzite.

There are some general criteria for which selected rocks are appropriate to become stones. These criteria are succinctly summed up in the following paragraph from *Building Stones of Our Nation's Capital*:

> When choosing a building stone, architects and planners use three characteristics to judge a stone's suitability: It should be pleasing to the eye; it should be easy to quarry and work; and it should be durable. Today it is possible to obtain fine building stone from many parts of the world, but the early builders of the city [Washington, D.C.—author] had to rely on materials from nearby sources. It was simply too difficult and expensive to move heavy materials like stone before the development of modern transportation methods like trains and trucks.[154]

In the first iteration of the Capitol, Aquia Creek sandstone satisfied these criteria. After the fire in 1814, when Benjamin Latrobe required a more beautiful stone for the columns in the new Senate and House Chambers, Potomac Marble replaced it. As a result, the fluted sandstone columns of the Jefferson-Latrobe House Chamber were replaced by the "beautifully magnificent" Potomac Marble columns we can admire today.

Chapter 16

QUARRYING AQUIA CREEK SANDSTONE

For the first iteration of the Capitol, sandstone was procured from the Aquia Creek Quarry. You may remember that the fluted columns that held up Thomas Jefferson's glass ceiling were constructed of Aquia Creek sandstone. This sandstone is also known as Virginia freestone because it is very easy to work with and cleaves in any direction. (See page 70.)

As early as 1791–92, Pierre Charles L'Enfant, the original designer of Washington, arranged for the government to purchase Higginston Island near Aquia, Virginia, in Stafford County for sandstone quarrying. It is now called Government Island. One advantage of government ownership was that local quarries were forced to keep their prices low in competition with the public quarry.[155] However, government ownership did not last for more than a few years, and the quarry was soon back in private hands.

In all, Aquia Creek sandstone was used for public buildings between 1790 and 1840, including the White House, Capitol, Treasury and Old Patent Office, which is now the National Portrait Gallery. The quarries were located not only on Government Island but also spread throughout Stafford County, where many can still be visited today.[156]

The sandstone here consists principally of quartz sand, pebbles and clay pellets cemented by silica. Interestingly, "the stone is unique because only here are the Coastal Plain sediments in the vicinity of Washington cemented sufficiently to be useful as a building stone."[157] In other words, in the early days of the Republic, builders were quite fortunate to have

Virginia freestone, as other sources of stone soon to be discovered were in the Piedmont, up the Potomac River, locked safely behind the Great Falls and Little Falls barriers.

Here is Latrobe's description of the sandstone from a report to President Jefferson on December 22, 1805:

> *The freestone of Aquia used in public buildings is a calcareous sand stone of very excellent quality, and the quarries are in appearance inexhaustible. It is however subject to clay-holes, to nodules of iron ore (pyrites) and to masses of flint, and the hardness and durability of the rock is often very various, in the same stratum. It also suffers expansion and contraction from moisture and dryness to a greater degree than any stone with which I am acquainted. Even after a block is taken out of the quarry, and delivered in the City, and in some cases after it has been wrought, it is liable to fly to pieces, if rapidly dried by violent heat or wind. But if it once becomes dry, and remains sound, it has never been known afterwards to fail.*[158]

The Aquia Creek Quarry on Government Island is located near the Potomac River about forty-five miles downriver from Washington, D.C., in Stafford County, Virginia. It is now a well-maintained county park and is worth a visit. It appears today as if the quarry workers had just laid down their tools for lunch, and it is easy to imagine the *thwack, thwack, thwack* of the hammers against the chisels.

Besides the ease with which Virginia freestone can be worked, the other advantage of these quarries was their location near the Potomac. Nowadays, Route 95 takes you right to the quarries from the capital, but in 1817, there was, of course, no Route 95. Rather, the river served as the highway. Upriver, from Point Lookout (where the Potomac River meets the Chesapeake Bay), the Potomac remained navigable, and even the largest nineteenth-century ships could sail all the way up past Alexandria and Washington to Georgetown. Just beyond Georgetown, though, is the fall line, where the Coastal Plain meets the Piedmont. Here, Little Falls and then Great Falls stood in the way of farther upriver navigation.

There were multiple quarrying methods used at these quarries, including "grooving and lofting" and "wedge notching."[159] The grooving and lofting method, often called "channeling,"[160] is the one I will discuss here, as it is the method you will most likely see on a visit to the Government Island quarries. Later on, I will let Latrobe himself describe the "wedge notching" method.

Aquia Creek Quarry at Government Island, Stafford County. The white stick is one meter in length.

A map showing the route from Washington, D.C., to the Aquia Creek Quarry at Government Island. *Google Earth Pro.*

How Aquia Creek sandstone was quarried. (The pole is one meter high for context.)

Let's use the picture above to help us understand how Aquia Creek sandstone was quarried using the grooving and lofting or channeling method.

First, workers removed the debris from the top portion of the rock and, using hammers, chisels and pickaxes, carved a vertical face (1). Then two channels, approximately twenty-three inches wide, were chiseled on each side (2) and in the rear (3). Now the block of stone was connected to the ground only at the bottom, and a worker could easily navigate around the block. Horizontal grooves were then carved with chisels at approximately the height of the building stone required (4). Finally, multiple wedges were inserted in the horizontal grooves and sequentially tapped by a hammer. As the wedges increased pressure on the stone, it eventually broke off, usually quite evenly.

In an article for the American Philosophical Association in 1809 titled "An Account of the Freestone Quarries on the Potomac and Rappahannoc," Latrobe describes the "wedge method":

> *In working these quarries, the workmen having cut the face perpendicularly, first undermine the rock; an easy operation, the substratum being loose sand.*

If the block is intended to be 8 feet thick, they undermine it 5 feet, in a horizontal direction, in order that it may fall over when cut off. They then cut two perpendicular channels on each hand, 1 ft. 6in. wide, at the distance from each other of the length of their block, having then removed the earth and rubbish from a ditch or channel along the top of the rock, they cut into the rock itself, a groove, and put in wedges along its whole length. These wedges are successively driven, the rock cracks very regularly from top to bottom, and it falls over, brought down partly by its own weight. Blocks have been thus quarried 40 feet long, 15 feet high, and 6 feet thick.[161]

To clarify what Latrobe is describing here, think of a stick of butter as the sandstone. When the stick is sliced by a knife, the pat of butter separates from the stick and falls over.

Whatever method was used, the cut stone was lifted by pulley and placed on a wheel-less skid called a "stone boat." It was then dragged by oxen to Aquia Creek along the "stone road," where it was put on scows or flat-bottomed barges, floated to the Potomac River, loaded onto schooners and

Sandstone from Government Island was dragged by oxen to Aquia Creek along this "stone road," where it was put on scows or flat-bottomed barges, floated to the Potomac River, loaded onto schooners and sailed upriver to Washington.

sailed upriver to Washington. Note that even with water transportation, the size of the sandstone blocks had to be limited to four tons each, according to Latrobe.[162]

Notice that because Aquia Creek sandstone is a freestone and easy to split, only the basic quarrying tools of hammers, chisels, pickaxes and wedges were needed to work the stone.

The Doric columns in the Capitol's crypt were carved from Aquia Creek sandstone. (See page 71.) The crypt was intended to be Washington's burial place, but he and later his family insisted on interment at Mount Vernon.[163] The fact that these columns have supported the ceiling for over two hundred years is a testament to their strength and durability, but looking more closely at them (below), you can see their imperfections.

When Latrobe returned to Washington, D.C., to begin rebuilding the Capitol, it appeared that the rebuild would be easier than the prewar construction. The population of the area was larger; supplies such as lime were more plentiful; and bridges, roads and canals had been constructed. All that was needed was freestone.[164] Latrobe's first inclination was to reopen the

A close-up of an Aquia Creek sandstone Doric column in the crypt. Notice the chisel marks and the discoloration.

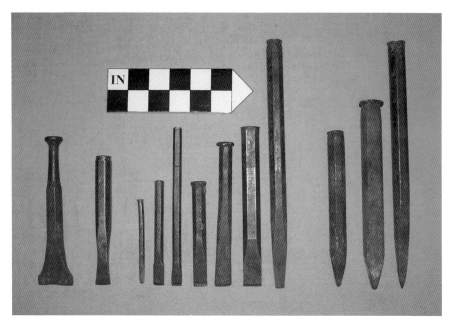

An assortment of chisels used by quarrymen in the nineteenth century. *Courtesy of Mary Gage and James Gage, www.stonestructures.org.*

quarries at Aquia Creek, but he was quite disappointed, as he wrote to in a report to the Senate on November 28, 1816:

> *To repair the public buildings generally, large Supplies of Freestone were necessary. The Quarries which are situated 40 miles below the city on the Patowmac, had been neglected for some Years, and time and much Labor were required to open them. Contracts were made by the proper officers for the freestone with several persons, proprietors of the old quarries, and new Quarries were opened and engaged in the supply.* **But as yet no Stone equal in quality, and as fit for the most important parts of the Work, as that formerly produced, has been found in any old or new Quarries** [author emphasis] *and as far as the work has proceeded, stone of coarser texture has unavoidably been employed; strength and durability being the only qualities that could be attended to.*[165]

Ultimately, Aquia Creek sandstone was not "of a texture fit for the finer works of buildings"[166] that would be required for the rebuild in 1817.

Another continual annoyance at this quarry, and others, was finding skilled stonemasons and laborers. During the early nineteenth century, cities such as New York, Baltimore and Philadelphia were all constructing stone buildings. For example, New York City Hall was completed in 1811, and the Baltimore Cathedral, designed by Latrobe, was begun in 1806. Having the choice to work in urban centers like New York or Baltimore or in the undeveloped Washington, D.C., meant that Latrobe often had an unenthusiastic workforce.

This problem was exacerbated by Congress, which was not sufficiently flexible to provide funding at the time that workers were set to be hired. As Latrobe explained it, quarry laborers were traditionally hired on January 1, and on that day, the best laborers were available. After that date, most of the workers hired would be second-rate but nevertheless more expensive because they knew they had you over a barrel. Yet Congress did not provide funds until much later in the year. Here was the result, as reported to Congress on December 22, 1805, by Latrobe:

> *In respect to common laborers, and to almost all the building artisans who have been brought up in this neighborhood, unless they can be engaged and employed during the winter, they cannot be depended upon until some time in July. In March the fishing season commences for shad and herrings, and lasts till the middle of May. Every man who has not profitable employment in hand, or who is not under engagements, then resorts to the shores. As soon as the fishing season is over the harvest commences, and until the end of the harvest, no great exertions, which depend upon these numerous classes of our people, can be made.*[167]

All kinds of other labor problems besides shortages, including strikes and accidents, plagued both the quarry and the construction site.

Chapter 17

QUARRYING POTOMAC MARBLE AND MORE

*U*nlike Aquia Creek sandstone, Potomac Marble is not a freestone and does not cleave very easily. The rock does fulfill at least two of the three criteria for stone; it is, when polished, beautiful and it is durable, but, as Latrobe was to quickly find out, quarrying was extremely difficult. In fact, you may remember that earlier in the book I described Potomac Marble as a "stonemason's nightmare." Quarrying requires different methods from Aquia Creek sandstone.

The quarry did have access to the Potomac River. In fact, as Latrobe said, "It overhangs the River, and would furnish <u>without any land carriage</u> all the Columns of the Capitol of one block each if required."[168] He was able to say this because the historical blockages to upriver navigation, Little Falls and Great Falls, had now been canalized; Little Falls in 1795 and Great Falls in 1802. If the river was deep enough, boats could pass down from the quarry to Washington, D.C., quite quickly.

Unfortunately, just as production was starting, Latrobe reported on July 24, 1817, "The locks of the Potowmac lower Canal [Little Falls] have fallen in, beyond the power of Art to restore them, we suffer difficulty in getting down our *Columbian* Marble; but a great effort will be made to bring them thence by Land."[169] Those arrangements must have been made because on August 12, 1817, Latrobe wrote, "I have now at the Capitol Nine blocks of Columbian Marble nearly finished for the Columns of the Hall of Representatives. I have never seen anything so beautifully magnificent."[170]

To extract large pieces of stone, the quarry workers began by drilling multiple holes along the line where they wanted to split the rock. Then, depending on various factors, they used explosives or splitting tools to force a split along the line of those holes. In the piece of Potomac Marble shown on the facing page, quarried over two hundred years ago, you can clearly see the drill holes on a regular path approximately the same distance apart, and in the picture below, you can see the drill holes in the moss-covered quarry wall.

The tool used to drill these holes is called a star drill, so called because of its star-shaped tip. The star drill required at least two people, and sometimes three, to be used efficiently. The man with the hammer was called a Jack, and if there were two people hammering, it was said that they were "double Jacking." The person holding the star drill was called the "shaker."

While the shaker held the star drill, the Jack would slam it with his eight-pound hammer. The shaker would then turn the drill a third of the way, and again, the hammer would fall. The shaker would turn the drill another third, and again, the hammer would fall. The shaker would turn the drill another third, and again, the hammer would fall.

Opposite: Latrobe quarry wall with drill holes. The pole is one meter high for context.

Above: A cut piece of Potomac Marble from Latrobe's quarry with drill holes. The pole is one meter high for context.

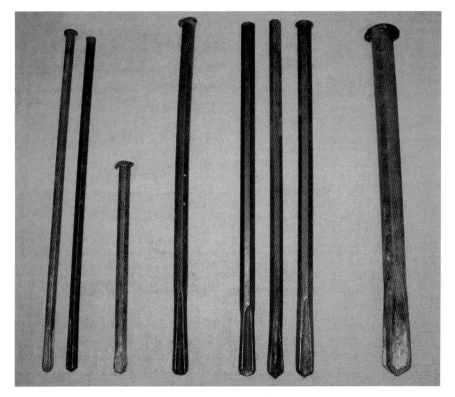

Above: An assortment of star drills used by quarrymen in the nineteenth century. *Courtesy of Mary Gage and James Gage, www.stonestructures.org.*

Opposite: Double Jacking the star drill. The shaker turns the drill after each hammer blow. Notice the row of holes already drilled. *National Park Service.*

This rhythm continued as the drill was driven deeper into the rock, only interrupted from time to time by the shaker, whose job it was to clear the dust out of the growing hole. When the hole was shallow, the shaker could just blow the dust out of it. As the hole deepened, the shaker might put some water in the hole to create mud, which would adhere to the drill and could be removed. As the hole deepened even more, the shaker might use a "deep hole mud spoon," which was essentially a small spoon with a really long handle.[171]

Once the hole was judged sufficiently deep, the process would begin again with another hole drilled nearby. This process continued hour after hour, day after day.

Drillers were paid a salary and then a bonus of one penny for each inch drilled. I don't know what the shakers were paid, but according to one

Different models of drills.

nal Park Service,
: Richard Schecht

researcher, the team was expected to drill about sixty inches, or five feet, per day. Apparently, many exceeded that.[172]

Once the row of holes was drilled, the workers may have used a flat wedge or a "wedge and feathers" to break the rock off from the main face. In the case of the latter, the "feathers" were inserted into each drill hole, and then the wedge was placed between the feathers. The quarry worker then hit each wedge sequentially, increasing the pressure on the rock, until it broke along the path of the drilled holes.

It is not clear to me which method, flat wedge or wedge and feathers, was used at the Latrobe quarry. According to *The Art of Splitting Stone*, which documents early quarrying methods in New England, the wedge and feathers was not introduced until 1823 in that area.[173] This would

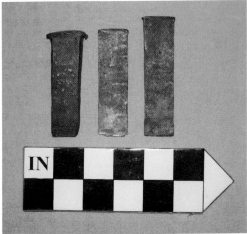

Top, left: A deep hole mud spoon made from a nail used by the shaker to remove debris from the drill hole. *Courtesy of Mary Gage and James Gage, www.stonestructures.org.*

Top, right: A selection of flat wedges used by quarrymen in the nineteenth century. *Courtesy of Mary Gage and James Gage, www.stonestructures.org.*

Bottom, left: On the left is a wedge and feathers used by quarrymen in the nineteenth century. *Courtesy of Mary Gage and James Gage, www.stonestructures.org.*

Bottom, right: Wedge and feathers inserted into drill holes. The quarryman will hit each wedge in sequence until the rock splits. *Courtesy of Connecticut Stone, Milford, Connecticut, www.connecticutstone.com.*

point to the flat wedge method in use at the Latrobe quarry in 1817. Thus, we have a minor mystery that perhaps can be solved by those who are expert in quarrying techniques (unlike myself). It is possible, though, that in parts of the quarry explosives were used, and I will discuss that a bit later in the chapter.

You may not be aware of this, but the star drill is a large part of American folklore. For example, in the famous folk song "John Henry":

> *John Henry said to his captain,*
> *"A man ain't nothing but a man.*
> *But before I let your steam drill beat me down*
> *I'll die with a hammer in my hand, Lord, Lord!*
> *I'll die with a hammer in my hand."*

What is John Henry doing? He is drilling a hole with a star drill in competition with a more modern steam drill. Here's the second verse:

> *John Henry said to his shaker,*
> *"Shaker, boy, you better start to pray,*
> *'Cause if my twelve-pound hammer miss that little piece of steel,*
> *Tomorrow'll be your burying day, Lord, Lord*
> *Tomorrow'll be your burying day."*

This is my favorite verse of the song because it answers the first question that comes to mind when thinking about a star drilling team: "What happens if the guy with the hammer misses?" Well, now we know!

It is probably true that the events of the John Henry song are taking place later than the period we are exploring. It has been suggested that John Henry was part of the crew that carved out the tunnels for the C&O Railroad in the 1870s.[174] But the star drill is the same tool then and even now. By the way, if John Henry *actually* used a twelve-pound hammer then he was a magnificently strong man!

We should not forget the Irish and Scottish drillers in the song "Drill Ye Tarriers, Drill":

> *Early in the morning at seven o'clock*
> *There are twenty tarriers drilling at the rock*
> *The boss comes around and he says, "Keep still,*
> *Come down heavy on your cast iron drill.*
> *And drill, ye tarriers, drill."*
> *Well, you work all day for the sugar in your tay*
> *Down beyond the railway*
> *And drill, ye tarriers, drill*
> *And blast, and fire.*

The "cast iron drill" is, of course, the star drill.

Now both John Henry and our tarriers are drilling holes for blasting rock, a very dangerous occupation now and even more so in the early nineteenth century, when the "blowers" used black powder. They did not use Alfred Nobel's dynamite, which was invented much later in the century. Dynamite is quite superior to black powder. It is super-sonic and very stable. Black powder is sub-sonic (less powerful) and very unstable. It is not for naught that Alfred Nobel named his explosive after the Greek word for power, *dynamis*.[175]

The drillers would pack the black powder into the star drill hole, tamp it down and insert a narrow metal pipe. The hole was then covered with wax or clay and the metal pile removed, leaving a hole for the fuse. Safety fuses were invented in 1831, so it is possible that the heroes of our songs used them, but certainly Latrobe's quarrymen did not. The purpose of safety fuses was to guarantee that a blower could escape the blast. Essentially, it was a rope wound around black powder that burned at the rate of thirty seconds per foot. If you wanted three minutes to clear the area before the powder went off, you would use six feet of safety fuse. Before the safety fuse was invented, though, the blowers used paper or straw as a fuse. If the area was wet, the fuse often soaked in grease to ensure its flammability. They would insert one end of the paper or straw into the fuse hole left by the pipe and light the other end—and then run.[176] As Joel Achenbach writes in his book *The Grand Idea*, "It took a great deal of finesse to drill a hole in solid rock, pack it with powder, insert a hollow iron rod, tamp some clay on top, insert a fuse, light it, and somehow get out of the way before the explosion launched boulders into the air."[177]

If the paper burned uniformly, the blowers would be able to escape, but there were many gory accidents. A newspaper report described one poor soul: "His situation is scarcely to be described, having the forepart of his head blown to pieces, one of his eyes blown out, and his breast and limbs shockingly bruised and mangled."[178] During the period under our consideration, a blower was paid the same as a laborer and was apparently not compensated for the danger of his occupation.[179]

There is one more quarrying tool I would like to discuss because it is quite clever. It is called a Lewis pin or Lewis. Apparently, no one knows if the Lewis pin was named after a man named Lewis or if Lewis is derived from some other ancient name or function. The device allows quarry workers to easily pick up large stones. It is known that the Lewis dates back 2,500 years. According to one author, the "Romans made extensive use of the Lewis, and introduced it into Europe and the British Isles."[180]

The Lewis pin is an ancient device used for lifting stones. The two blades are put in a hole in the stone, and when the ring is pulled, they separate and the stone can be lifted. *Cathetus at the English-language Wikipedia, creativecommons.org/licenses/ by-sa/3.0, via Wikimedia Commons.*

The Lewis pin has two scissor-like arms attached to a chain. When the chain is pulled, those two toothed arms pivot away from each other. If the Lewis pin is inserted into the hole in a stone and pressure is exerted on the chain, the arms will each lock on to the side of the hole in the rock, and the rock can be lifted by its own weight. You may remember that, according to Latrobe, when George Blagden, the master stonemason, was trying to dissuade President Monroe from employing Potomac Marble, "he [Blagden] reported in writing, that the stone would not bear its own weight, when lewis'ed. I immediately suspended by a small Lewis a block of 2 ton weight in the Capitol."[181]

It bears repeating that Potomac Marble was very difficult to quarry and very difficult to work with. Here is Samuel Lane, commissioner of public buildings, describing the quarry difficulties in a letter to a congressman:

> *After the most flattering prospects, we had frequently to encounter unexpected disappointments. A large block, quarried with great expense of time and labor, and promising to furnish the whole residue of the columns, would often turn out to be full of dry veins, and in working would fall to pieces; when another part of the quarry would be tried, perhaps, with no better success.*[182]

And here, in 1851, a reporter from the *Alexandria Gazette and Virginia Advertiser* relates how difficult working with the stone was back in 1817:

> *Much care was necessarily required in shaping the noble columns, owing to the brittleness of the material. While one workman directed the chisel, which he held by a withe,[183] another struck the blow with a sledge hammer. The comparatively few flaws—which could not be avoided—were filled in with colored sealing wax. The polishing was executed with sand, emery and putty, rubbed on with woollen cloths. The columns are in seven or eight*

THIS SANDSTONE WAS ORIGINALLY PART OF THE UNITED STATES CAPITOL'S EAST FRONT, CONSTRUCTED IN 1824-1826. IT WAS QUARRIED BY LABORERS, INCLUDING ENSLAVED AFRICAN AMERICANS, AND COMMEMORATES THEIR IMPORTANT ROLE IN BUILDING THE CAPITOL.

Above: This piece of sandstone on display at the Capitol has a hole in the center so that it can be lifted with a Lewis pin.

Left: A sign indicating the history of the sandstone block from the previous picture.

pieces but the joints are well fitted as to convey the impression that they were taken, full length from the quarry.[184]

As a result of such difficulties, the Hall of Representatives was not completed until 1819, and instead of $1,550, the highest estimate for the cost of a column, it actually amounted to something like $5,000.[185]

If you look closely at one of the columns in the old House Chamber today, you can see the imperfections, but only close up. You can see the

In this close-up of a Potomac Marble column from the Old House Chamber, you can see the seams between the "drums" composing the column and the black wax infill where a clast has fallen out of the matrix.

seam between the sections that compose the column and the black wax that is used to fill area where a clast has fallen out of the matrix. But if you see them as they were meant to be seen, composing a beautiful space, then the imperfections are invisible (see page 67).

The Potomac Marble quarry along the Potomac was developed with great speed due to the pressing need to complete the Capitol. In 1817, much to President Monroe's frustration, Congress was still meeting in temporary quarters. After General Swift and Colonel Bomford returned from their inspection of the quarry, they wrote in a letter to the president on March 31, 1817:

> *Let one hundred good men and a leader be procured from New-York or Boston, and sent to Washington, to work upon the capitol. Let the architect employ two good draughtsmen to prepare triplicates of all plans and such other drawing as may be required.... To expedite the work at the quarry, we recommend, that, in addition to the men that may be procured in and about Washington, Baltimore, Georgetown, and the vicinity of the quarry, let there be hired*

and sent on from Philadelphia, thirty or forty quarry men, and twenty stone cutters—from New-York the same numbers. Captain Reese can attend to the procuring of the men at Philadelphia—Gen. Swift, at New-York.[186]

On April 4, 1817, in a letter to Samuel Lane, President Monroe micromanaged the long-delayed project in an attempt seemingly to "just get it done, already!" Notice the last sentence of the letter, which is put in bold for emphasis:

Let Mr. Latrobe employ two good draftsmen to assist him in preparing his drafts and estimates. A division of labour is equally necessary in respect to the columns. It divides itself, naturally into two parts, the getting the stone from the quarry and the shaping it afterwards. Mr. Leckie[187] *will take charge particularly of the first, and Mr. Hartnet*[188] *of the second, and you will procure for each, as many workmen as can be advantageously employed in his branch. Mr. Leckie will deliver over the blocks to Mr. Hartnett.*

You will provide tools, lumber, nails, spikes and provisions, for Mr. Leckie, who will cause sheds to be erected for the workmen, for cooking and as store houses without delay. The provisions ought to be issued, at proper stated periods, and returns and receipts to be kept of them.

You must pay the workmen every week of which rolls and receipts should be kept.

You may employ a clerk at the quarry, who on your responsibility, shall take charge of the provisions and pay the workmen, keeping regular accounts thereof.

You will report to me every Monday morning, the progress of the work in concise terms, in every branch of the public works.[189]

The location of the Potomac River quarry, while excellent from the standpoint of transportation, was pretty much a wilderness. There were no shops nearby, and everything had to be provided for the workers, including housing, food and, in the case of the hired slaves, clothes. As Samuel Lane wrote in a report to Congress:

The quarry being situated in a country where no accommodation could be had for the workmen, imposed on me the necessity of purchasing materials and erecting temporary huts, of laying in provisions, utensils for cooking, bedding, & etc., and, in some instances, clothing for servants, hired of their masters with that condition.[190]

Also required were work areas for blacksmiths who maintained the quarrymen's tools, other shops and provisions for whatever animals were needed.

Nevertheless, progress was made, and Latrobe reported to Jefferson on June 28, 1817, "There are now 100 men, laborers & Stone cutters at work in the Quarry." Additionally, "There are now 9 blocks here [Washington, D.C.] from 6 to 8 feet long each. Three of them make one Column. They are rounded, but not yet polished."[191]

PART V

THE QUARRY AND THE RIVER

*It overhangs the River, and would furnish without any land carriage
all the Columns of the Capitol.*

—*Benjamin Latrobe, August 8, 1815*

Chapter 18

ODE TO THE RIVERMEN

*A*s I wrote earlier, the Potomac River is navigable from the Chesapeake Bay to Georgetown. Here at the fall line, where Coastal Plain meets the Piedmont, are two barriers that prohibit further navigation: Little Falls and Great Falls. Great Falls drops seventy-six feet in less than a mile, and Little Falls drops thirty-six feet.[192] It was George Washington's strategic vision that the river should be made navigable, eventually providing a link to the Ohio River. Latrobe wrote of a 1798 meeting with Washington: "The conversation then turned upon the rivers of Virginia, He [G.W.] gave me a very minute account of all their directions, their natural advantages, and what he conceived might be done for their improvement by art."[193] Washington believed that without roads and rivers connecting Ohio and the West to the East, the people of the West were liable to break from the United States and either form an independent nation or be absorbed by European powers still operating on the continent.

Additionally, connecting the new Capital City to the West would help it develop into an urban center that manufactured and distributed raw materials coming in from the West. Washington knew that industrialization was not compatible with the feudal slave labor policies of his state and other southern states. Perhaps here was a way to undermine and eventually destroy slavery. In 1795, he set up the Potomac Company to achieve these purposes.

Initially lacking the skilled labor needed to build locks, the company sent squads of workers up the Potomac and its tributaries. Blasting away the impediments to navigation, they attempted to improve the river by "removing

The Potomac River is difficult to navigate under normal conditions, a situation that Washington's Potomac Company sought to resolve. For example, in this area of the river near Harpers Ferry, no boat could pass without a sluice or until after spring freshets. *Courtesy of Roger Biraben.*

the rocks." By and large, they were successful. Sluices and bypasses were created in shallow areas, and boats, directed by buoys chained to submerged rocks in the river, could successfully negotiate down the Potomac and its tributaries under certain conditions. (See page 79.) Unfortunately, those conditions existed only about fifty days a year when the spring freshets or rains raised the water level of the river.[194]

Boatmen, their boats loaded with stone, wheat, coal and other products of the area, waited in groups along the banks of the Potomac and its tributaries for conditions to be right. They smoked and swore, told stories and lies, played games and sang songs, developing a short-lived river culture that is little remembered today:

> *These boats were pleasant places of resort, and at night around each blazing fire would be seen groups engaged in playing "seven-up," "hustle cap," or the sly game of "two pluck one," matching pennies. Now and then a strong voice would break out in a love-ditty which would be echoed far up the river.*[195]

As soon as the rain came, they shot downstream, navigating the man-made sluices and bypass canals guided by the chained buoys. These boats were often seventy feet long and about nine feet wide. They had a crew of four: one man in the stern operating the rudder, two polemen on each side and one in the bow.[196] Having often witnessed myself how terrifying the Potomac River is during high water, I can only admire the great skill and bravery of these boatmen.

Having reached Georgetown, their freight delivered, the boats were either sold or laboriously poled back up the river. In fast water, the boatmen used the buoy chains[197] or strategically placed capstans to drag themselves along.

The Little Falls locks were opened in 1795 and the Great Falls locks in 1802. Until that time, boats unloaded at Great Falls and rolled their barrels down an inclined plane, where they were reloaded and brought farther downriver.[198]

By 1817, the locks around Great Falls and then Little Falls had been working for years. Latrobe wrote of the Potomac Marble quarry, "It overhangs the River, and would furnish without any land carriage all the Columns of the Capitol."[199] Here he is referring to the ability of boats to float right down to Washington uninterrupted because of the Great Falls and Little Falls locks. There was a bit of a hiccup, however. In July 1817, exactly at the point when the Potomac Marble quarry was going full blast, the locks at Little Falls collapsed. Marble could still be brought by boat through the Great Falls locks to Little Falls, where it was loaded on wagons for the rest of the way to Washington.

I often lead expeditions to my discovery, the Latrobe quarry. Visitors are sometimes initially disappointed, expecting a large hole in the ground. But Latrobe's quarry was a quarry in the air and not in the ground. Most of the quarry was destroyed when the C&O Canal was built, but you can still stand on its remaining edges today, seventy-five feet in the air, and look up and down the Potomac River imagining those riverboats and their courageous crews at high water shooting down the roaring river to the Great Falls and Little Falls locks and on to the capital.

CONCLUSION

To the perpetual union of the United States. It has already saved us
in the times of storm, one day it will save the world.
—Marquis de Lafayette, 1824

Benjamin Latrobe never completed the Capitol building. Constantly under pressure from President Monroe, Samuel Lane and Congress, the work he accomplished was often judged unfairly. William Lee, a diplomat and client of Latrobe's, wrote:

> *Latrobe has many enemies; his great fault is being poor. He is, in my*
> *opinion, an amiable, estimable man, full of genius and at the head of his*
> *profession. Every carpenter and mason thinks he knows more than Latrobe,*
> *and such men have got on so fast last year with the President's house (a*
> *mere lathing and plastering job) that they have the audacity to think they*
> *ought to have the finishing of the Capitol; a thing they are totally unfit for.*
> *That superb pile ought to be finished in a manner to do credit to the country*
> *and the age.*[200]

Additionally, Latrobe was seldom able to get along with coworkers, especially those vested with more authority than he, and this was especially true with his boss, Samuel Lane: "The present Commissioner, Colonel Lane, has from the first week, treated me as his clerk, & certainly not with the delicacy with which I treat my mechanics."[201] Meanwhile, impatient with the progress of the Capitol rebuild, President Monroe organized a meeting with Lane and Latrobe in the presidential chambers on November 20, 1817. For Latrobe, this meeting could not have happened at a less opportune time. Informed of his son Henry's death from yellow fever in New Orleans only a month earlier, he was still suffering from deep depression. Additionally, he was dead broke and hadn't paid his rent in months. When he was reprimanded by Lane at the meeting:

> *Something in him snapped; it was too much for his harried nerves to bear. Latrobe leaped at Lane and, as reported years later by his wife, "seized him by the collar, and exclaimed, 'Were you not a cripple, I would shake you to atoms, you poor contemptible wretch! Am I to be dictated to by you?' The President said looking at my husband, 'Do you know who I am, Sir?' 'Yes, I do and ask your pardon, but when I consider my birth, my family, my education, my talents, I am excusable for any outrage after the provocation I have received from that contemptible character.'"*[202]

Latrobe resigned on November 20, 1817, sending President Monroe the following letter:

> *My situation as architect of the Capitol has become such as to leave me no choice, but between resignation and the sacrifice of self-respect. Permit me then sire to resign into your hands an office in which I fear I have been the cause to you of much vexation while my only object has been to accomplish your wishes. You have known me more than twenty years: you have borne testimony to my professional skill and my integrity has never been in question. You will, I am confident, do me justice, and, in time, know, that never the delay nor the expense of the public works are chargeable to me.*[203]

The president accepted the resignation and hired Charles Bullfinch of Boston. Among Bullfinch's earlier projects was his beautifully designed State House in Boston. Bullfinch continued to work on the Capitol until its completion in 1830.

In 1820, Latrobe moved to New Orleans to complete the drinking water system for which his son Henry, following in his father's Philadelphia footsteps, had been the engineer. Tragically, on September 3, 1820, the father suffered the same fate as the son, dying of yellow fever while attempting to complete Henry's work. Benjamin Latrobe was buried in the city's Protestant cemetery. Biographers agree that the grave may have been marked originally, but now the location is unknown.[204]

This memorial was installed at the New Orleans Protestant cemetery by descendants of Latrobe, father and son, who succumbed to yellow fever while building a city water system. *Courtesy of historicaldilettante.blogspot.com/2012/06/the-latrobe-family.html.*

About a year before his death on March 6, 1819, Latrobe wrote the following in his journal:

> *I remember the time when I was over head & ears in love with* Man *in a state of nature. By the bye, I never heard any fine theory spun together in behalf of* Women *in a state of nature.* Social Compacts *were my hobbies, the American revolution (I ask its pardon, for it deserves better company) was a sort of dawn of the golden age, and the French revolution the Golden Age itself. I should be ashamed to confess all this if I had not had a thousand companions in my kaleidoscopic amusement, and those generally men of ardent, benevolent, & well-informed minds, & excellent hearts. Alas! Experience has destroyed the illusion, the kaleidoscope is broken, and all the tinsel of scenery that glittered so delightfully is tarnished & turned to raggedness. A dozen Years of residence at the republican court of Washington has assisted wonderfully in the advance of riper Years.*[205]

The statement is humorous and insightful but tinged with bitterness and pathos. Disappointed with what he was able to achieve, he writes as a sad old man though only in his fifties. If only he knew that more than two hundred years after his death, we would still be writing of his genius.

As far as I can determine, Potomac Marble was used only once in a significant project, and that was in 1817 through 1820 in the Capitol, although one geologist claims that the quarry was reopened from time to time through the nineteenth century.[206] Jim O'Connor, former Washington, D.C. geologist, referring to the House Chamber, writes that Potomac Marble's "only claim to fame was this room."[207] The stone proved difficult to work with. Single columns could not be quarried, so columns were usually assembled from three or more pieces, and the expense of the beautiful columns soared.

BUT ALL OF THIS *is relatively unimportant.*

What *is* important is that the British attempt to demoralize and dissolve the young United States of America failed. In a few short years, we went from the "magnificent ruin" of 1814 to the classic treasure pictured in Samuel F.B. Morse's 1822 painting.

In this grand hall, history—our history, American history, good and bad—continued to be made until 1857, when a new House Chamber was constructed for a growing Congress.

It was here that the Revolutionary War hero Marquis de Lafayette became the first foreign dignitary to address the House of Representatives on December 10, 1824. Here is his optimistic response to a toast from Congress: "To the perpetual union of the United States. It has already saved us in the times of storm, one day it will save the world."[208]

It was here that former president John Quincy Adams, as congressman from 1831 to 1848, battled the slaveocracy control of Congress using both wiles and wit. Adams, of course, also had a secret weapon. Due to the unusual acoustical characteristics of the chamber, he could hear the quiet conversations of his adversaries across the room.[209] It was also here that this ardent opponent of evil suffered a fatal stroke at his desk on the House floor and died two days later on February 23, 1848, in the Speaker's room just off the hall of the House.[210]

It was here that the young Abraham Lincoln in 1847 issued his "Spot Resolution." A mere freshman congressman, he challenged the proslavery President Polk to show him the "spot" where the Mexican army had supposedly attacked American soldiers. In a moment similar to the 2003 "Weapons of Mass Destruction" debacle, the proslavery forces lied to provoke a war with Mexico to seize land for the expansion of slavery.[211]

It was here that the abominable Indian Removal Act was passed on May 26, 1830, by a vote of 101 to 97. This led directly to the tragic Trail of Tears forced resettlement of tens of thousands of American Indians to reservations in the West.

This floor plaque indicates the location of John Quincy Adams's desk in the old House Chamber. Fortuitously, due to unusual acoustics, he was able to overhear the opposition proslavery discussions across the room.

A drawing depicting the death of J.Q. Adams after a stroke while at his desk in the Old House Chamber. *Architect of the Capitol.*

A floor plaque indicating the location of Congressman Abraham Lincoln's desk. It is from this position that he gave his famous "Spot Resolution" speech. *Architect of the Capitol.*

Finally, it was here that the representatives of the American people debated and voted for almost forty years and where Abraham Lincoln, Davy Crockett, Henry Clay, Stephen A. Douglas and many others made their first appearances on the national scene.

AS THE NUMBER OF states and their representatives increased, there were discussions about what to do with the superannuated House Chamber. Suggestions that it be used as an art gallery were soon dismissed, as the walls are obscured by the columns.

Finally, on April 19, 1864, Representative Justin S. Morrill asked: "To what end more useful or grand, and at the same time simple and inexpensive, can we devote it [the chamber] *than to ordain that it shall be set apart for the reception of such statuary as each State shall elect to be deserving of in this lasting commemoration?" His proposal to create a National Statuary Hall became law on July 2, 1864.*[212]

Here is the relevant section of that law:

The President is hereby authorized to invite each and all the States to provide and furnish statues, in marble or bronze, not exceeding two in number for each State, of deceased persons who have been citizens thereof, and illustrious for their historic renown or for distinguished civic or military services such as each State may deem to be worthy of this national commemoration; and when so furnished the same shall be placed in the Old Hall of the House of Representatives, in the Capitol of the United States, which is set apart, or so much thereof as may be necessary, as a national statuary hall for the purpose herein indicated.[213]

By 1933, as the statuary became excessively crowded, a new law was passed that reduced the number of statues for each state to a single statue, and the remaining were placed in other parts of the Capitol. There have been more rearrangements over the decades and, in recent times, a number of removals. As history progresses and the national temperament changes, these statues will come and go; but the Potomac Marble columns remain, and perhaps, like those of the Parthenon in Athens, they will be proclaimed a wonder of the world in two thousand years.

NOTES

Introduction

1. Bowles, *Stone Industries*, 5.

Chapter 1

2. Chaitkin, *Who We Are*, 16n7. Latrobe studied under civil engineer John Smeaton, who founded the Society of Civil Engineers and was active earlier in Benjamin Franklin's circles in England before the American Revolution.
3. "I detest the morality of the English government, by far the most unprincipled and cruel of modern times in its conduct to foreign nations, and the most unjustifiably so, as she pretends to uncommon humanity, justice and religion." Van Horne, *Papers of Benjamin Henry Latrobe*, vol. 3, *1811–1830*, 693. Letter from Latrobe to Thomas Johnson, January 4, 1813. Johnson was the former governor or Maryland now operating iron furnaces.
4. Chenoweth, "Most Beautiful Room in the World?," 29. For more about Latrobe and jazz, see www.frenchcreoles.com/ArtTheater/Congo%20 Square/congo%20square.html.
5. Hamlin, *Benjamin Henry Latrobe*, 76. Hamlin quotes from Latrobe's Manuscript Journal, vol. 1, pp. 58ff. Maryland Historical Society.

6. Description of the visit to George Washington derived from the following sources: Carter, Van Horne and Brownell, *Latrobe's View of America*, 6; Hamlin, *Benjamin Henry Latrobe*, 75; Baker, *Building America*, 2–3.

7. The steam engines were purchased from Nicholas Roosevelt of New York City. Roosevelt was fourth great-grandfather of Theodore Roosevelt and later became Latrobe's son-in-law.

8. Witcher, "Philadelphia Municipal Water Supply"; Documentary History of American Water-works, "Philadelphia, Pennsylvania"; Carter, Van Horne and Brownell, *Latrobe's View of America*, 6.

9. American Philosophical Society. "The first woman was elected in 1789— the Russian Princess Dashkova, president of the Imperial Academy of Sciences of St. Petersburg."

10. Hamlin, *Benjamin Henry Latrobe*, 1133–34.

11. Standiford, *Washington Burning*, 241.

12. Padover, *Thomas Jefferson and the National Capital*, 299. Jefferson letter to Latrobe, March 15, 1803.

13. Architect of the Capitol, www.aoc.gov/explore-capitol-campus/ buildings-grounds/capitol-building/history.

14. This summary portrait of Latrobe's early life and education is drawn from many sources but, in particular, two biographies of Latrobe: Hamlin, *Benjamin Henry Latrobe*; Baker, *Building America*.

15. Padover, *Thomas Jefferson and the National Capital*, 390; Latrobe letter to Jefferson, May 21, 1807.

16. Chenoweth, "Most Beautiful Room in the World?," 28.

17. Latrobe, *Anniversary Oration*, 10.

18. Ibid., 11.

19. Baker, *Building America*, 83.

20. Hamlin, *Benjamin Henry Latrobe*, 294. Quoting letter from Latrobe to Lenthall on May 3, 1805. Lenthall is Latrobe's assistant.

21. Van Horne, *Papers of Benjamin Henry Latrobe*, vol. 2, *1805–1810*, 693. Letter from Latrobe to Hazlehurst, January 16, 1809. Hazlehurst is Mary Latrobe's father.

22. Hamlin, *Benjamin Henry Latrobe*, 272.

23. The Library of Congress was initiated by President Adams, who asked Congress for a $5,000 authorization to purchase books in 1800. See www. loc.gov/about/history-of-the-library.

24. Chenoweth, "Most Beautiful Room in the World?" 23.

25. Ibid., 32.

26. Ibid., 29.

27. Standiford, *Washington Burning*, 243.

28. Hamlin, *Benjamin Henry Latrobe*, 556. According to Hamlin, Latrobe wrote an article in *The Edinburg Encyclopedia* on acoustics in 1812; it was not published until 1832.

29. Allen, *History of the United States Capitol*, 71–72.

30. Hamlin, *Benjamin Henry Latrobe*, 267.

31. Van Horne, *Papers of Benjamin Henry Latrobe*, vol. 2, *1805–1810*, 215. Letter from Latrobe to Peale, April 18, 1806.

32. Hamlin, *Benjamin Henry Latrobe*, 269.

33. Le Libellio d' AEGI, Vol. 8, n2 (Été 2012): 67–74, lelibellio.com/wp-content/uploads/2013/02/vol.-8-n%C2%B0-2-pages-67-%C3%A0-74-Chenoweth-R.-The-very-first-Miss-Liberty....pdf.

34. Padover, *Thomas Jefferson and the National Capital*, 470–71. Jefferson letter to Latrobe, July 12, 1812.

35. "Ingraham, a former ship captain from Massachusetts who had served on board the *Bonhomme Richard* in its famous encounter with the *Serapis*, was a New York City shipowner, merchant, and land speculator." founders.archives.gov/documents/Hamilton/01-25-02-0188.

36. Van Horne, *Papers of Benjamin Henry Latrobe*, vol. 3, *1811–1820*, 480. Letter from Latrobe to Ingraham, September 9, 1813.

Chapter 2

37. Snow, *When the British Burned the White House*, 11.

38. Taylor, *Internal Enemy*.

39. Ibid., 129.

40. Ibid., 28. During the Revolution, "6,000 Virginia slaves had fled to the British, but only about one third obtained their freedom by evacuation to the British colony of Nova Scotia. Another third died during the war, primarily of disease. The final third reverted to their masters after Cornwallis abandoned."

41. Ibid., 3, 28, 29, 37, 128, 179, 246.

42. Atkinson, *British Are Coming*, 352–56.

43. Taylor, *Internal Enemy*, 209.

44. War of 1812, www.warof1812.ca/trousers.htm.

45. Pitch, *Burning of Washington*, 34.

46. Michigan Weather Center, "Tornado and the Burning of Washington."

47. Taylor, *Internal Enemy*, 300.

48. Anthony Pitch, "Patriotism and the Reconstruction of Washington, D.C., after the British Invasion of 1814," in Valie and Capanella, *Resilient City*, 97. "Washington, D.C. in 1814, was a steamy southern backwater with a population of only 8,000 residents, one-sixth of whom were slaves."

49. United States Capitol Historic Society, *Capitol Dome* 51, no. 3 (Fall 2014): 13.

50. Pitch, *Burning of Washington*, 100.

51. Ibid., 19.

52. Standiford, *Washington Burning*, 228, 258–59.

Chapter 3

53. Congreve rockets; Jamil, "Why Mysore?"; Van Sickle, *Congreve Rockets*; Military History Fandom, "Congreve Rocket."

54. Pitch, *Burning of Washington*, 109.

55. Van Horne, *Papers of Benjamin Henry Latrobe*, vol. 3, *1811–1820*, 670. Letter from Latrobe to Jefferson, July 12, 1815.

56. Pitch, *Burning of Washington*.

57. United States Congress, *Documentary History*, 172. Madison to Congress, November 20, 1814.

58. Standiford, *Washington Burning*, 287.

59. Chenoweth, "Most Beautiful Room in the World?," 10.

60. Brown, *History of the United States Capitol*, 39.

61. Pitch, *Burning of Washington*, 20.

62. Valie and Capanella, *Resilient City*, 98.

63. *Capitol Dome* 51, no. 3 (Fall 2014): 40. Extract from "Conflagration of Washington" by Philip Freneau.

64. Lance Humphries, "Who Dubbed Baltimore the 'Monumental City'?" *Baltimore Sun*, August 15, 2015, www.baltimoresun.com/opinion/op-ed/bs-ed-monument-city-20150815-story.html.

65. As a somewhat ironic afterword to these events, those who burned down the capital, General Ross and his troops, were mostly Irish born, and when the capital was rebuilt, it was Irishmen who did it. Over half the population of Washington, D.C., at this time was Irish, most of whom spoke only Gaelic. See *Capitol Dome* 51, no. 3 (Fall 2014): 10.

Chapter 4

66. United States Congress, *Documentary History*, 174.
67. There was even a suggestion that the Capitol be built at the intersection of the Potomac River and the Monocacy River because that was above the fall line and impossible for warships to reach. I am glad this never happened, in particular, because it is one of my favorite fishing haunts for smallmouth bass.
68. United States Congress, *Documentary History*, 176–77.
69. Ibid., 181.
70. Pitch, "Patriotism and the Reconstruction of Washington, D.C.," 107.
71. United States Congress, *Documentary History*, 182.
72. Ibid., 175; House proceedings of October 20, 1814: Annals of Congress, 13—3, p. 413.
73. United States Congress, *Documentary History*, 185.
74. Hamlin, *Benjamin Henry Latrobe*, 434.
75. Pitch, *Burning of Washington*, 120. Pitch extracts this from Klapthor, "Benjamin Latrobe and Dolley Madison Decorate the White House."
76. Hamlin, *Benjamin Henry Latrobe*, 435.
77. Carter, Van Horne and Brownell, *Latrobe's View of America*, 334. The Tuscan order was developed by the Romans and is similar to the Greek Doric order.

Chapter 5

78. History, Art and Archives, United States House of Representatives.
79. Pitch, *Burning of Washington*, 48.
80. Van Horne, *Papers of Benjamin Henry Latrobe*, vol. 3, *1811–1820*, 712. Letter from Latrobe to Charlotte Ann Francis Bloom, who was an old friend from England, November 20, 1815.
81. Ibid., 776.
82. *National Intelligencer*, January 24, 1817. Latrobe letter to the editor dated January 18, 1817. Library of Congress, newspaper collection: "It is now about twenty years ago since I observed in visiting that part of Virginia which lies immediately below the southwest mountain, a Breccia or Bedding Stone, scattered in large masses."
83. American State papers, Class 10, Misc. II 428F. Latrobe Report to Committee on Public Buildings: November 28, 1816.

84. *National Intelligencer*, January 24, 1817. Latrobe letter to the editor dated January 18, 1817. Library of Congress.
85. American State papers, Class 10, Misc. II 434. Abstract of disbursements by Samuel Land, Commissioner of Public Buildings between April 30 and October 1, 1816, on account of contingent expenses, page 434.
86. Ibid., Class 10, Misc. II 511F. Samuel Lane report to Committee on the Expenditures of the Public Buildings, January 24, 1818.
87. Ibid., Class 10, Misc II 428F. Latrobe report to Congress, February 18, 1817.
88. Ibid., Class 10, Misc II 511F. Samuel Lane report to Committee on the Expenditures of the Public Buildings, January 24, 1818.
89. Pitch, "Patriotism and the Reconstruction," 110. See footnotes 51–56.
90. See description of a Lewis pin on pages 126–27.
91. Padover, *Thomas Jefferson and the National Capital*, 482. Latrobe letter to Jefferson, June 28, 1817.
92. A special thank-you to Erin's Marble and Granite of Sterling, Virginia. Despite their hesitations, they cut and polished my first sample of Potomac Marble, revealing how beautiful a stone it is.
93. Chaitkin, *Who We Are*, 189–204.
94. Kapsch, *Building Washington*, 119.
95. United States Congress, *Documentary History*, 220–21. Letter from Monroe to Swift & Bomford, March 17, 1817.
96. Swift, *Memoirs*, 149–50. Note that William C. Allen in his *History of the United States Capitol* says the quarry visit was March 28, not March 25.
97. Allen, *History of the United States Capitol*, 110–17.
98. United States Congress, *Documentary History*, 198. Letter from President Monroe to Samuel Lane, April 4, 1817.
99. Van Horne, *Papers of Benjamin Henry Latrobe*, vol. 3, *1811–1820*, n877. Letter from Latrobe to Swift and Bomford, March 31, 1817.
100. Ibid., 905. Letter from Latrobe to Thomas Jefferson, June 28, 1817.
101. Padover, *Thomas Jefferson and the National Capital*, 489. Latrobe letter to Jefferson, August 12, 1817.
102. United States Congress, *Documentary History*, 199. President Monroe's Annual Message, December 12, 1817.

Chapter 6

103. Padover, *Thomas Jefferson and the National Capital*, 482. Latrobe letter to Jefferson, June 28, 1817.
104. Architect of the Capitol.

Chapter 7

105. Ramsburg, *Report on Potomac Marble*, 9.
106. Bowles, *Stone Industries*, 168. "From a commercial standpoint, all limestones capable of polish are considered marble."
107. Lee and Froelich, *Triassic-Jurassic Stratigraphy*, 19.
108. Roberts, *Geology of the Virginia Triassic*, 11.
109. Lee and Froelich, *Triassic-Jurassic Stratigraphy*, 19.
110. Van Horne, *Papers of Benjamin Henry Latrobe*, vol. 1, *1784–1804*, 162–63. Letter from Latrobe to Robert Goodloe Harper, April 24, 1800. Harper was a Revolutionary soldier, close friend and former congressman.
111. Ibid., vol. 3, *1811–18204*, 719–21. Letter from Latrobe to Nathaniel Macon, January 9, 1816. Macon was a Republican congressman from North Carolina.
112. Watson, *Mineral Resources of Virginia*, 69: "At Goose Creek the marble bed is about 62 feet thick and has been worked to a considerable depth. These beds are pure, and the stone is of great beauty, and takes a good polish; thus far, however, the lack of transportation has prevented extensive quarrying."
113. Roberts, *Geology of the Virginia Triassic*, 11–12.
114. American State papers, Class 10, Misc II 428F. Latrobe Report to Committee on Public Buildings, November 28, 1816.
115. Roberts, *Geology of the Virginia Triassic*, 129.
116. Lee and Froelich, *Triassic-Jurassic Stratigraphy*, 19.

Chapter 9

117. Scheel, "History of Loudoun's Limestone Overlay District."

Chapter 10

118. American State papers, Class 10, Misc II 428F. Latrobe Report to Committee on Public Buildings, November 28, 1816.

119. Ibid., Image 434, *Abstract of Disbursements Made by Samuel Lane*, December 12, 1816.

120. The Samuel Clapham estate, Chestnut Hill, still stands off Route 15 on Chestnut Hill Lane in northern Loudoun County. Having received permission from the current owners to look around, I saw no Potomac Marble outcrops remaining. Those that did exist were probably removed to aid farming.

121. Hamlin, *Benjamin Henry Latrobe*, 444. The story told by John H. Latrobe is reported on page 64 of his autobiography, *John H. Latrobe and His Times*. The apocryphal nature of the story is that John says that it was at the Clapham estate that his father "saw for the first time the Breccia from which the columns of the House of Representatives... were afterward obtained." However, Benjamin Latrobe in his January 18, 1817 letter to the *National Intelligencer* says, "It is now about 20 years" since he first noticed Potomac Marble.

122. Kapsch, *Building Washington*, 218.

123. Allen, *History of the United States Capitol*, 106.

124. Norton, *Latrobe, Jefferson and the National Capitol*, 241.

125. Taylor, *Memoir of Loudoun County*, 8–9.

126. *Maryland Geological Survey*, 187–193.

127. Roberts, *Geology of the Virginia Triassic*, 130.

128. Department of Interior, *Building Stones of Our Nation's Capital*, 12. Please note three errors in this text: I have seen no evidence that Potomac Marble was brought to the Capitol after 1820, and the C&O Canal was not opened until 1828. Furthermore, when Potomac Marble was sent to Washington, D.C., it was shipped via the Potomac River.

129. Ibid., 8.

130. C&O Canal Trust, "Marble Quarry Campsite."

Chapter 11

131. Scheel, "History of Loudoun's Limestone Overlay District."

132. Thank you to my friend Master Angler David Crenshaw of Leesburg, Virginia, for helping me measure the depth of the pond using his Deeper Sonar device.

133. The photographs were provided to me by Dan Davis, the education director of the Loudoun County Izaak Walton League. He received them in a letter dated March 10, 2015, from Tom Caviness, whose father, Jack Caviness, was a charter member of the organization.
134. Scheel, "History of Loudoun's Limestone Overlay District."

Chapter 12

135. In 2020, I chanced upon the owner of the property while I was snooping around for rock samples. I asked his plans for the land, and he indicated that low quality of the landfill used to fill the quarry was presenting problems for development.
136. Roberts, *Geology of the Virginia Triassic*, 128.
137. History of Loudoun County, Virginia, "African American Communities."
138. The information sign at the site says the quarry opened in 1868. Scheel, "History of Loudoun's Limestone Overlay District." Scheel says it opened in 1888 and closed in 1945.

Chapter 13

139. *Genius of Liberty*, April 8, 1817. Thank you to historian Edward Spannaus of the Lovettsville Historical Society for locating this advertisement.
140. Scheel, "In Debate About Documents' Hiding Place."
141. *National Intelligencer*, January 24, 1817. Library of Congress newspaper collection. Latrobe letter to the editor, January 18, 1817.
142. Van Horne, *Papers of Benjamin Henry Latrobe*, vol. 3, *1811–1820*, 681. Letter from Latrobe to the Commissioners of Public Buildings, August 8, 1815.
143. American State Papers, Miscellaneous, Volume II, 427. Benjamin Latrobe, letter to Congress, November 28, 1816: "The present Commissioner of the public buildings has, therefore, entered into a contract for all the columns and progress has been made in quarrying them."
144. Carter, Van Horne and Brownell, *Latrobe's View of America*, 336.
145. Ramsburg, *Report on Potomac Marble*, 1.1.
146. Camp Kanawha has a six-foot-high Potomac Marble obelisk near its gate and uses the stone for some of its building's chimneys. This is the only structural use of Potomac Marble besides the columns in the Capitol

that I have so far seen. I am indebted to Dr. George Lewis for guiding me through this area.

147. *National Intelligencer*, January 24, 1817. Library of Congress newspaper collection. Letter to the editor dated January 18, 1817.

148. On the successful second attempt on November 18, 2018, I was accompanied by Dr. Roger Biraben of Hillsboro, Virginia, who aided me in the search for the quarry.

149. Ramsburg, *Report on Potomac Marble*, 1 Although Ramsburg says that there was "no trace of blue overlying limestone described by Latrobe," I did find some bluestone scattered on the floor of the quarry.

150. These stones were first noted by historian and journalist Jon Wolz.

151. Note that as of winter 2022, White's Ferry remains closed. An alternative is to begin upriver at the Dickerson Conservation Park entrance to the towpath and walk downriver about two miles until you reach Mile Post 38.

Chapter 14

152. National Archives II: Inventory of the National Park Service, Volume 1 of 3, Record Group 79, Entry Number P/E 298, Boxes 1 & 2, Stack 150, Row 36, Compartment 9, Shelf 5.

153. Ibid.

Chapter 15

154. Withington, *Building Stones of Our Nation's Capital*, 2.

Chapter 16

155. Norton, *Latrobe, Jefferson and the National Capitol*, 43, 88.

156. For the complete history of the Virginia freestone quarries in Stafford County, see MacGregor and Eby, *Great Rock of Aquia*.

157. Department of Interior, *Building Stones of Our Nation's Capital*, 8.

158. Van Horne, *Papers of Benjamin Henry Latrobe*, vol. 2, *1805–1810*, 172. Footnote in a Latrobe report to Jefferson on December 22, 1805.

159. MacGregor and Eby, *Great Rock of Aquia*, 87.

160. Gage and Gage, *Art of Splitting Stone*, 21.

161. Latrobe, "Account of the Freestone Quarries," 291. Thanks to James Gage, who sent me a link to this article, part of which he quotes in his book, *Art of Splitting Stone.*

162. Department of Interior, *Building Stones of Our Nation's Capital*, 9.

163. If you are able to arrange a personal tour of the Capitol from your congressional representative, as I did, ask to see Abraham Lincoln's catafalque, stored beneath the crypt.

164. Kapsch, *Building Washington*, 216.

165. Van Horne, *Papers of Benjamin Henry Latrobe*, vol. 3, *1811–1820*, 832. Report on the U.S. Capitol, November 28, 1816.

166. Ibid., 851.

167. United States Congress, *Documentary History*, 115. Latrobe to Congress, December 22, 1805.

Chapter 17

168. Van Horne, *Papers of Benjamin Henry Latrobe*, vol. 3, *1811–1820*, 682. Latrobe to the Commissioners of Public Buildings, August 8, 1815.

169. Padover, *Thomas Jefferson and the National Capital*, 485. Latrobe letter to Jefferson, July 24, 1817.

170. Ibid., 487–89. Latrobe letter to Jefferson, August 12, 1817.

171. Wood, *Tools and Machinery*, 45.

172. Kapsch, *Potomac Canal*, 213–14.

173. Gage and Gage, *Art of Splitting Stone*. See Editor's Note section without page numbers, "Revised Dating for Plug & Feathers Method and Flat Wedge Method."

174. National Park Service, "John Henry."

175. Achenbach, *Grand Idea*, 134.

176. *Handbook of Mining Details*, 26–27; Achenbach, *Grand Idea*, 134; Kapsch, *Potomac Canal*, 214.

177. Achenbach, *Grand Idea*, 134.

178. Ibid., 325fn134.

179. Kapsch, *Potomac Canal*, 214.

180. Gage and Gage, *Art of Splitting Stone*, 60fn111.

181. Padover, *Thomas Jefferson and the National Capital*, 482. Latrobe letter to Jefferson, June 28, 1817.

182. United States Congress, *Documentary History*, 220. Samuels to Congressman Cobb, December 20, 1819.

183. Dictionary, "withe," www.dictionary.com/browse/withe: "an elastic handle for a tool, to lessen shock occurring in use."

184. "Marble Columns of the Hall of Representatives," *Alexandria (VA) Gazette and Virginia Advertiser*, November 8, 1851. Thank you to William Bauman and Jon Wolz for forwarding this article to me.

185. United States Congress, *Documentary History*, 220. Samuels to Congressman Cobb, December 20, 1819.

186. Ibid., 222–23. Letter from Swift to Monroe, March 31, 1817.

187. Robert Leckie was the director of U.S. Arsenals and a former quarryman.

188. John Hartnet was an experienced marble mason.

189. United States Congress, *Documentary History of the Construction and Development of the United States Capitol Building and Grounds*, 198. Letter from Monroe to Lane, April 4, 1817.

190. American State papers, Class 10, Misc II 511F, Samuel F. Lane to Congress, January 24, 1818.

191. Padover, *Thomas Jefferson and the National Capital*, 481–82. Latrobe letter to Jefferson, June 28, 1817.

Chapter 18

192. Wikipedia, "Patowmack Canal."

193. Hamlin, *Benjamin Henry Latrobe*, 76. Quoted from Latrobe's journal.

194. Gutheim, *Potomac*, 252–53.

195. Kapsch, *Potomac Canal*, 260. Quoted from Thomas and Williams, *History of Allegany County*, 206.

196. Kapsch, *Potomac Canal*, 253–58.

197. Gutheim, *Potomac*, 254.

198. Kapsch, *Potomac Canal*, 90–91.

199. Van Horne, *Papers of Benjamin Henry Latrobe*, vol. 3, *1811–1820*, 681–82. Letter from Latrobe to the Commissioners of Public Buildings, August 8, 1815.

Conclusion

200. Van Horne, *Correspondence and Miscellaneous Papers*, vol. 3, *1811–1820*, 954n5. Letter from William Lee to Charles Bullfinch, October 21, 1817.

201. Padover, *Thomas Jefferson and the National Capital*, 491. Letter from Latrobe to Jefferson, November 20, 1817.
202. Hamlin, *Benjamin Henry Latrobe*, 477. Quoted by Hamlin from a memoir by Mary Latrobe. See fn 10, page 477.
203. Van Horne, *Correspondence and Miscellaneous Papers*, vol. 3, *1811–1820*, 968–69. Letter from Latrobe to Monroe, November 20, 1817.
204. Baker, *Building America*, 226.
205. Carter, Van Horne and Formwalt, *Journals of Benjamin Henry Latrobe*, 239.
206. Roberts, *Geology of the Virginia Triassic*, 130. "The so-called 'Potomac' marble or 'calico rock' has been quarried at intervals near Point of Rocks, Maryland for something over a century and a quarter but these quarries have not been operated for about 30 years."
207. Robbins and Welter, "Building Stones," 16.
208. Woodward, *Lafayette*, 428.
209. Miller, *Arguing about Slavery*. This wonderful book tells the story of J.Q.A.'s battles in Congress.
210. United States House of Representatives, History, Art & Archives.
211. The Spot Resolution: www.loc.gov/resource/mal.0007000/?st=text.
212. Architect of the Capitol, "The National Statuary Hall Collection," www.aoc.gov/explore-capitol-campus/art/about-national-statuary-hall-collection.
213. Ibid.

BIBLIOGRAPHY

Books and Periodicals

Achenbach, Joel. *The Grand Idea*. New York: Simon and Schuster, 2004.

Allen, William C. *The History of the United States Capitol*. 106th Congress, 2d Session, Senate Document, 2005.

Atkinson, Rick, *The British Are Coming*. New York: Henry Holt & Company, 2019.

Baker, Jean H. *Building America: The Life of Benjamin Henry Latrobe*. New York: Oxford University Press, 2020.

Bowles, Oliver. *The Stone Industries*. London: Forgotten Books, 2018.

Brown, Glenn. *History of the United States Capitol*. New York: Da Capo Press, 1970.

Carter, Edward C., II, John C. Van Horne and Charles E. Brownell, eds. *Latrobe's View of America, 1795–1820*. New Haven, CT: Yale University Press, 1985.

Carter, Edward C., II, John C. Van Horne and Lee W. Formwalt, eds. *The Journals of Benjamin Henry Latrobe, 1799–1820*. New Haven, CT: Yale University Press, 1980.

Chaitkin, Anton. *Who We Are*. Self-published, 2020.

Chenoweth, Richard. "The Most Beautiful Room in the World? Latrobe, Jefferson and the U.S. Capitol." *The Capitol Dome*, "Special Edition: Examining the War of 1812," 51, no. 3 (Fall 2014).

Chesapeake and Ohio Canal: A Guide to Chesapeake and Ohio Canal National Historical Park. Washington, D.C.: Government Printing Office, 1991.

Fairman, Charles E. *Art and Artists of the Capitol of the United States of America*. Washington, D.C.: United States Government Printing Office, 1927.

Gage, Mary, and James Gage. *The Art of Splitting Stone: Early Rock Quarrying Methods in Pre-Industrial New England, 1630–1825*. Amesbury, MA: Powwow River Books, 2005.

Geological Survey Professional Paper 147. Washington, D.C.: United States Government Printing Office, 1989.

Gutheim, Frederick. *The Potomac*. New York: Rinehart & Company, 1949.

Hamlin, Talbot. *Benjamin Henry Latrobe*. New York: Oxford University Press, 1955.

———. *The Pennsylvania Magazine of History and Biography*, April 1941.

Jennings, Paul. *Colored Man's Reminiscences of James Madison*. Brooklyn, NY: George C. Beadle, 1865.

Kapsch, Robert J. *Building Washington*. Baltimore, MD: Johns Hopkins University Press, 2018.

———. *The Potomac Canal*. Morgantown: West Virginia University Press, 2007.

Klapthor, Margaret Brown. "Benjamin Latrobe and Dolley Madison Decorate the White House." *Smithsonian Museum United States National Museum Bulletin* 41 (1966).

Latrobe, B. Henry. "An Account of the Freestone Quarries on the Potomac and Rappahannoc Rivers." *Transactions of the American Philosophical Society* 6 (1809): 291.

———. *Anniversary Oration, Pronounced before the Society of Artists of the United States: by Appointment of the Society, on the Eighth of May, 1811*. Sabine Americana, Print Editions 1500-1926.

Lee, K.Y., and AJ. Froelich. *Triassic-Jurassic Stratigraphy of the Culpeper and Barboursville Basins, Virginia and Maryland*. U.S. Geological Survey Professional Paper 1472, 1989.

MacGregor, Alaric, III, and Jerrilynn Eby. *The Great Rock of Aquia*. Berwyn, MD: Heritage Books, 2021.

Maryland Geological Survey. Vol. II. Baltimore, MD: Johns Hopkins Press, 1898.

Miller, Lillian B., ed. *The Peale Family: Creation of a Legacy, 1770–1870*. Washington, D.C.: National Portrait Gallery, 1996.

Miller, William Lee. *Arguing about Slavery: The Great Battle in the United States Congress*. New York: Alfred A. Knopf, 1996.

National Park Service. *Chesapeake and Ohio Canal*. Washington, D.C.: National Park Service, 1991.

Norton, Paul. *Latrobe, Jefferson and the National Capitol.* New York: Garland Publishing Company, 1977.

Padover, Saul K., ed. *Thomas Jefferson and the National Capital.* Washington, D.C.: United States Government Printing Office, 1946.

Pitch, Anthony S. *The Burning of Washington.* Annapolis, MD: Naval Institute Press, 1998.

Poland, Charles P., Jr. *From Frontier to Suburbia.* Marceline, MO: Walsworth Publishing Company, 1976.

Ramsburg, Owen H. *Report on Potomac Marble.* Washington, D.C.: United States Congress, Architect of the Capitol, Records, Office of the Curator, Capitol Stone files, 1965.

Roberts, Joseph K. *The Geology of the Virginia Triassic.* Charlottesville: University of Virginia, 1928.

Scheel, Eugene. "In Debate about Documents' Hiding Place, a Loudoun Legend Lives On." *Washington Post*, August 18, 2002. www.washingtonpost.com/archive/local/2002/08/18/in-debate-about-documents-hiding-place-a-loudoun-legend-lives-on/d39e399b-816c-48b7-9627-4480e4c98e73.

Semmes, John E. *John H. Latrobe and His Times, 1803–1891.* Baltimore, MD: Norman, Remington, Co., 1917.

Snow, Peter. *When the British Burned the White House.* New York: Thomas Dunne Books, St. Martin's Press, 2014.

Standiford, Lee. *Washington Burning.* New York: Three Rivers Press, 2008.

Swift, Joseph Gardner. *The Memoirs of Gen. Joseph Gardner Swift, LLD., U.S.A., First Graduate of the United States Military Academy, West Point, Chief Engineer U.S.A. from 1812–1818, 1800–1865.* N.p.: Wentworth Press, 2016.

Taylor, Alan. *The Internal Enemy.* New York: W.W. Norton & Company, 2013.

Taylor, Yardley. *Memoir of Loudoun County, Virginia.* Leesburg, VA: Thomas Reynolds, 1853.

Thomas, James W., and Thomas J.C. Williams. *History of Allegany County, Maryland.* Cumberland, MD: L.R. Titsworth and Company, 1923.

United States Congress. House Commission on Construction of House Office Building. *Documentary History of the Construction and Development of the United States Capitol Building and Grounds.* Washington, D.C.: Government Printing Office, 1904.

Valie, Lawrence J., and Thomas J. Capanella. *The Resilient City.* New York: Oxford University Press, 2005.

Van Horne, John C., ed. *The Correspondence and Miscellaneous Papers of Benjamin Henry Latrobe.* Vol. 3, *1811–1820.* New Haven, CT: Yale University Press, 1988.

————. *The Papers of Benjamin Henry Latrobe*. Vols. 1–3. New Haven, CT: Yale University Press, 1988.

Van Sickle, Eugene. *The Congreve Rockets in the War of 1812*. Dalton, GA: Bandy Heritage Center, Dalton State College, n.d.

Watson, Thomas Leonard, PhD. *Mineral Resources of Virginia*. Lynchburg, VA: J.P. Bell Company, 1907.

Witcher, T.R. "The Philadelphia Municipal Water Supply Was the First of Its Kind." *American Society of Civil Engineering Magazine*, January 2, 2021.

Withington, Charles F. *Building Stones of Our Nation's Capital*. Washington, D.C.: United States Government Printing Office, 1998.

Wood, Paul. *Tools and Machinery of the Granite Industry*. Newport, RI: Chronicle of Early American Industries Association, June 2006.

Woodward, W.E. *Lafayette*. New York: Farrar & Rinehart, 1938.

Web Pages

American Philosophical Society. www.amphilsoc.org/elected-members.

American Society of Civil Engineers. "The Philadelphia Municipal Water Supply Was the First of Its Kind." January 2, 2021. source.asce.org/the-philadelphia-municipal-water-supply-was-the-first-of-its-kind.

American State Papers. memory.loc.gov/ammem/amlaw/lwsp.html.

Architect of the Capitol. www.aoc.gov.

Baltimore Sun. www.baltimoresun.com.

Bandy Heritage Center for Northwest Georgia. www.bandyheritagecenter.org.

C&O Canal. "Marble Quarry Campsite." www.canaltrust.org/pyv/marble-quarry-campsite.

Congreve rockets. weebau.com/history/mysorean_rock.htm.

Department of Interior. *Building Stones of Our Nation's Capital*. Washington, D.C.: Department of Interior, 1975, 8. pubs.usgs.gov/gip/70039206/report.pdf.

Documentary History of American Water-works. "Philadelphia, Pennsylvania." www.waterworkshistory.us/PA/Philadelphia.

Handbook of Mining Details (1912). books.google.com/books?id=O1ROA AAAYAAJ&pg=PP2&lpg=PP2&dq=Handbook+of+Mining+Details +princeton&source=bl&ots=V93EkePZq8&sig=ACfU3U2rs0pNzPB 1c7_racHCMNtP-hx33w&hl=en&sa=X&ved=2ahUKEwi7-4y9htD2A hVcgnIEHbqvCFEQ6AF6BAgEEAM#v=onepage&q= Handbook%20of%20Mining%20Details%20princeton&f=false.

History, Art and Archives, United States House of Representatives. history.house.gov.

The History of Loudoun County, Virginia. "An Introduction to Loudoun County's African American Communities." www.loudounhistory.org/african-american-communities.

Jamil, Arish. "Why Mysore? The Idealistic and Materialistic Factors behind Tipu Sultan's War Rocket Success." *Emory Endeavors in History* (2013). history.emory.edu/home/documents/endeavors/volume5/gunpowder-age-v-jamil.pdf.

Loudoun County History. www.loudounhistory.org/history.

Michigan Weather Center. "The Tornado and the Burning of Washington, August 25, 1814." michigan-weather-center.org/the-tornado-and-the-burning-of-washington-august-25-1814.

Military History Fandom. "Congreve Rocket." military-history.fandom.com/wiki/Congreve_rocket.

National Park Service. www.nps.gov.

———. "John Henry and the Coming of the Railroad." www.nps.gov/neri/learn/historyculture/john-henry-and-the-coming-of-the-railroad.htm.

Robbins, Eleanora I., and Myrna H. Welter. "Building Stones and Geomorphology of Washington, D.C.: The Jim O'Connor Memorial Field Trip." May 4, 2001, 16. www.gswweb.org/oconnor-fieldtrip.pdf.

Roberts, Joseph K. *The Geology of the Virginia Triassic.* Charlottesville: University of Virginia, 1928. www.dmme.virginia.gov/commercedocs/BUL_29.pdf.

Scheel, Eugene. "History of Loudoun's Limestone Overlay District." www.loudounhistory.org/history/limestone-overlay-district.

United States Capitol Historic Society. *The Capitol Dome.* uschs.org/engage/read-the-capitol-dome.

Virginia Chronicle. virginiachronicle.com.

War of 1812. www.warof1812.ca/trousers.htm.

Washington Post. www.washingtonpost.com.

White House Historical Association. www.whitehousehistory.org.

Wikipedia. "Patowmack Canal." en.wikipedia.org/wiki/Patowmack_Canal.

INDEX

A

acoustics 21
Adams, John Quincy 142
American Philosophical Society 18, 19, 21, 34, 40, 44
Andrei, Giovanni 21
Aquia Creek Quarry 21, 30, 109, 110, 111, 112, 114, 115, 116, 117, 119
Architect of the Capitol 97
Armstrong, John 27

B

Basingstoke Canal 17
Bell, Chief Ranger 100
black powder 30, 126
Blagden, George 39, 40, 127
boats 39, 119, 136, 137
Bomford, Colonel George 40, 41, 129
breccia 49, 96, 100, 109

British 25, 26, 27, 28, 29, 30, 31, 37, 89, 126, 142
British logistics 26
Bullfinch, Charles 140

C

Campioli, Mario E. 97
Carlheim Manor 61
caverns 61
Caviness, Tom 86
Chenoweth, Richard 20, 22
Chesapeake and Ohio Canal 85, 97, 104, 105, 137
Clapham, Samuel 38, 83, 94, 95, 96
clasts 49, 50, 109
Cochrane, Alexander Vice Admiral 26
Cockburn, Rear Admiral George 25, 31
columns 21, 44, 116
commissioner of public buildings 35, 38, 83, 127

conglomerate 49, 50, 109
Congreve rockets 29, 31
crypt 116

D

deep mud hole spoon 122
dynamite 126

F

Franklin, Benjamin 18
Freneau, Philip 31
Fulton, Robert 34
fuses 126

G

Genius of Liberty 94
Georgetown, Maryland 112, 129,
135, 137
glass 30
Great Falls 112, 119, 135, 137
Greece 17, 18, 19, 44, 126

H

Hamlin, Talbot 83
Hartnet (Hartnett), John 38, 41, 94,
95, 130
House of Representatives 20, 21,
29, 34, 38, 41, 43, 44, 110,
128, 142, 144, 145

I

Ingraham, Nathaniel 24

J

Jefferson, Thomas 17, 19, 20, 21,
22, 24, 29, 30, 36, 37, 40, 42,
110, 111, 112, 131

K

karst 57, 60

L

Lafayette, Marquis de 142
Lane, Samuel 36, 38, 39, 83, 95,
127, 130, 139, 140
Latrobe, Benjamin Henry 15, 17,
18, 19, 20, 21, 22, 24, 29, 30,
32, 34, 35, 36, 37, 38, 39, 40,
41, 42, 43, 44, 49, 50, 83, 84,
85, 86, 95, 96, 100, 110, 112,
114, 115, 116, 118, 119, 123,
126, 127, 130, 131, 135, 137,
139, 140, 141
Latrobe, Mary 34
Leckie, Robert 39, 41
Leesburg Limestone Quarry 86
Leesburg, Virginia 30, 36, 49, 50,
56, 57, 60, 61, 63, 83, 84, 86,
90, 94, 95, 109
L'Enfant, Pierre Charles 111
Library of Congress 20, 30, 31
limestone 49, 50, 57, 61, 85, 86,
90, 93, 96, 109, 110
Lincoln, Abraham 142, 144
Little Falls 112, 119, 135, 137
Loudoun County 38, 41, 49, 50,
51, 56, 57, 61, 63, 81, 83, 84,
85, 86, 90, 94, 95
Luck Stone Quarry 50, 109

M

Madison, Dolley 35
Madison, James 27, 28, 30, 35, 36, 37
marble 21, 37, 38, 39, 41, 42, 47, 49, 50, 51, 56, 83, 85, 90, 95, 96, 97, 104, 110, 119, 144
Mason Island 96, 97
Monroe, James 28, 36, 39, 40, 41, 42, 127, 129, 130, 139, 140
Montgomery County 38, 41, 51, 81, 83, 85, 94
Morse, Samuel F.B. 44, 142
Museum of Curiosities 22

N

Napoleon 25, 26
Navy Yard 30
New Orleans 17, 140
New York 21, 22, 118

O

Oehrlein, Mary 97
Olde Izaak Walton Park 83, 86, 93

P

Parthenon 37, 42, 145
Peale, Charles Wilson 21, 22
Philadelphia, Pennsylvania 18, 19, 22, 34, 118, 130, 140
Point of Rocks, Maryland 41, 85, 97
Potomac Marble 37, 38, 39, 40, 41, 42, 43, 44, 46, 47, 49, 50, 51, 56, 57, 83, 84, 85, 86, 87, 89, 90, 95, 100, 104, 109, 110, 119, 120, 127, 129, 137, 141, 145
Potomac River 18, 25, 39, 49, 63, 83, 97, 112, 115, 119, 130, 135, 137

Q

quarry tools 26, 40, 112, 114, 116, 120, 122, 123, 125, 126, 127

R

Ramsburg, Owen H. 97, 100
republican 17, 19, 20
Republican 32
Roberts, Joseph K. 50, 84
Ross, General Robert 26
Rust, William 21

S

sandstone 21, 30, 37, 49, 104, 109, 110, 111, 112, 114, 115, 116, 117, 119
Scheel, Eugene 61, 86, 89, 90, 95
Senate Chamber 20, 44, 84, 97, 104
slavery 19, 25, 130, 135, 142
star drill 120, 125, 126
Statue of Liberty 21, 22
steam 18, 125
stonecutter 40, 42, 130, 131
stone mason 42, 118
Supreme Court 20
surveyor of public buildings 19
Swift, General Joseph Gardner 40, 41, 129, 130

T

Taylor, Yardley 84
Treaty of Ghent 31
Triassic period 49, 84
Tuscan order 36

W

War of 1812 25, 31
Washington, D.C. 18, 19, 22, 24,
      26, 27, 28, 32, 33, 34, 36, 37,
      39, 40, 41, 42, 50, 84, 85, 89,
      94, 95, 106, 110, 111, 112,
      116, 118, 119, 129, 131, 135,
      137, 141, 142
Washington, George 18, 19, 27, 28,
      32, 50, 135
water supply 18, 63
West Point 40
White House 19, 30, 35, 111

ABOUT THE AUTHOR

*P*aul Kreingold is a thirty-seven-year resident of Leesburg, Virginia, where he and his wife have raised two children. He is currently the president of the Banshee Reeks Chapter of the Virginia Master Naturalists and the conservation director of the Izaak Walton League, Loudoun County Chapter. His interest in geology and history dates back to his college days, but after a long career in computer system design, he has devoted his time in the last five years as a researcher and educator. Besides public lectures throughout Loudon, Montgomery and Frederick Counties, Kreingold regularly leads "expeditions" to the rediscovered Latrobe Potomac Marble quarry along the beautiful Potomac River.

Visit us at
www.historypress.com